PENGUIN CLASSICS

THE HUNTING OF THE SNARK

LEWIS CARROLL was the vigorously preserved pen-name of the Rev. Charles Lutwidge Dodgson. Born in 1832, he was educated at Rugby and Christ Church, Oxford, where he spent the rest of his life as lecturer in mathematics. In 1861 he took deacon's orders, but shyness and a constitutional stammer prevented him from seeking the priesthood. He never married but he was very fond of children and spent much of his time with them – the Alice books were originally written for the young daughters of Dr Liddell, the Dean of Christ Church. Besides his stories, Lewis Carroll also wrote nonsensical poems and parodies; in addition he published some learned mathematical treatises, but these were of little significance beside his brilliantly absurd fiction. His prose and verse works include: *Alice in Wonderland* (1865) and *Through the Looking-Glass* (1872), *Phantasmagoria and Other Poems* (1869), *The Hunting of the Snark* (1876), and *Sylvie and Bruno* (1889). Charles Dodgson died in 1898

MARTIN GARDNER was born in 1914 in Tulsa, Oklahoma. In 1936 he took his BA at the University of Chicago, majoring in philosophy, in which he went on to do some graduate work. He worked as a journalist and publicity writer up to the outbreak of the Second World War, during which he served in the United States Navy. Since then he has been a freelance writer. From 1957 to 1982 he wrote a monthly recreational mathematics column in *Scientific American*, which delighted a world-wide audience comprising mathematicians and dreamers, scientists and schoolchildren, computer programmers and poets. He has also contributed to the *Journal of Philosophy*, *Philosophy of Science*, *Philosophy of Phenomenological Research* and other philosophical journals. He edited and wrote the introduction to *The Moscow Puzzles* by Boris A. Kordemsky. His books *Mathematical Puzzles and Diversions*, *More Mathematical Puzzles and Diversions*, *Mathematical Carnival*, *Mathematical Circus* and *Mathematical Magic Show* are all published by Penguin, as well as *The Annotated Alice, The Annotated Snark* and *The Ambidextrous Universe*. Among his other published works are *Fads and Fallacies in the Name of Science, The Relativity Explosion, Logic Machines and Diagrams, The Annotated Ancient Mariner, Order and Surprise, The New Age, Science: Good, Bad and Bogus, How Not to Test a Psychic, The Whys of a Philosophical Scrivener* and *Gardner's Whys and Wherefores*.

Mr Gardner is married and has two sons. His main hobby is conjuring.

The Hunting of the Snark

AN AGONY IN EIGHT FITS

with the original illustrations by *Henry Holiday*

With an introduction and notes by

MARTIN GARDNER

PENGUIN BOOKS

PENGUIN BOOKS

Published by the Penguin Group
Penguin Books Ltd, 27 Wrights Lane, London W8 5TZ, England
Penguin Putnam Inc., 375 Hudson Street, New York, New York 10014, USA
Penguin Books Australia Ltd, Ringwood, Victoria, Australia
Penguin Books Canada Ltd, 10 Alcorn Avenue, Toronto, Ontario, Canada M4V 3B2
Penguin Books (NZ) Ltd, 182–190 Wairau Road, Auckland 10, New Zealand

Penguin Books Ltd, Registered Offices: Harmondsworth, Middlesex, England

First published in the USA by Bramhall House 1962
Published in this country by Penguin Books Ltd 1967
Reprinted with revisions 1974
Reprinted in Penguin Classics 1995
5 7 9 10 8 6 4

Designed by Ian E. Staunton
Printed in England by Clays Ltd, St Ives plc
Filmset in Monophoto Modern Extended Series 7

With love to

RACHEL OTT

Acknowledgements

I would like to thank the following persons for contributing in one way or another to the writing of this book: Stephen Barr, Everett Bleiler, Norman Brennan, Lin Carter, Roger Green, Norman Gridgeman, J. A. Lindon, Leigh Mercer, and Vincent Starrett. To Warren Weaver I am especially grateful for the loan of rare editions of *The Hunting of the Snark* from his incomparable Carroll collection, so that the best possible reproductions could be made of Holiday's illustrations; to my wife, a salaam for invaluable help, as always.

MARTIN GARDNER

CONTENTS

But, should the play
Prove piercing earnest,
Should the glee glaze
In Death's stiff stare,

Would not the fun
Look too expensive!
Would not the jest
Have crawled too far!

EMILY DICKINSON

PREFACE

for the Penguin Edition

It is a great privilege indeed to have Penguin reprint, as a companion to its edition of my *Annotated Alice*, this curious little commentary on Lewis Carroll's immortal nonsense poem, *The Hunting of the Snark*.

A complete resetting of type has made it possible to correct a few errors, update the bibliography, add new material to some of the notes, and to record in this preface some information I did not possess when I first wrote the book.

I did not know, for example, that the entire ballad, with the exception of the Barrister's Dream, had been set to music by Max Saunders and broadcast several times on the B.B.C. Third Programme in the early fifties. The 'sought it with thimbles' stanza was sung as a chorus by a choir of ten men, and the rest of the poem was sung or recited to orchestral accompaniment by Michael Flanders. Douglas Cleverdon was the producer. There has been talk from time to time of issuing this as a long-playing record, but so far nothing has come of it. On Christmas Eve, 1963, *The Hunting of the Snark* was read by Alec Guinness on the B.B.C. Third Programme, and this also has since been rebroadcast. The only recording of the *Snark* that I am aware of is a long-playing record of the Ballad read by Boris Karloff and released by Caedmon Company in 1959.

Nor did I know that Snark clubs have flourished at both Oxford and Cambridge, and that the Cambridge group still meets in London. The Oxford club, I am told by Michael H. Harmer, the Bellman (secretary) of the Cambridge group, was founded in 1879 at New College. Known as The Snarks, it met regularly during the 80s and 90s but apparently had its last official meeting in 1914 on the eve of the First World War. In 1952 someone found the club's address book and there was a dinner in London attended by about thirty-five guests, but that was the last gathering of the crew. John Galsworthy and A. P. Herbert were among the distinguished members. The *Observer*, in its colour supplement, 8 January 1967, page 6, printed an 1888 photograph of five members of The Snarks, showing young Galsworthy in the centre, sporting a monocle.

The Cambridge group was founded in 1934 by a group of medical students and has been meeting once a year ever since for dinner and a reading of the Agony. It has, at any one time, exactly ten members, each corresponding to a member of Carroll's Snark-hunting crew. The club's eleven rules are so delightfully Snarkish that, with the Bellman's permission, I reproduce them below:

1. That the Club be called the *Snark Club*.
2. That the object of the Club be the glorification of the Snark and its creator.
3. That an Annual Dinner shall be held.
4. That at each Annual Dinner the *Agony* be read complete.
5. That the fine for non-attendance at the Dinner be a *cheque drawn to bearer for seven pounds ten*, which shall be *crossed*.
6. That any member of the Crew who shall be separated from the scene of the Dinner by not less than *one thousand diminished by eight* nautical miles, be exempt from the fine mentioned in Rule 5.
7. That members be posted in the Agony Column of *The Times* newspaper after non-attendance at the Dinner exceeding two consecutive years.
8.
9. That members be replaced as they *softly and suddenly vanish away*.
10. That the Bellman be responsible for the upkeep of the bell, and that it be his peculiar privilege to tingle same.
11. That *Strange Creepy Creatures* may be admitted as additional

members of the Crew from time to time, provided the total number available for Snark service at any one time shall not exceed ten.

MARTIN GARDNER
Hastings-on-Hudson, New York

INTRODUCTION

Martin Gardner

ALTHOUGH Lewis Carroll thought of *The Hunting of the Snark* as
a nonsense ballad for children, it is hard to imagine – in fact one
shudders to imagine – a child of today reading and enjoying it.
Victorian children may have found it amusing (there is a grim
record of one little girl having recited the entire poem to Carroll
during a long carriage ride), but even they, one suspects, were few
in number.

'It is not children who ought to read the words of Lewis Carroll,'
writes Gilbert Chesterton, 'they are far better employed making
mud-pies.' Carroll's nonsense should be read by

sages and grey-haired philosophers . . . in order to study that darkest
problem of metaphysics, the borderland between reason and un-
reason, and the nature of the most erratic of spiritual forces, humour,
which eternally dances between the two. That we do find a pleasure
in certain long and elaborate stories, in certain complicated and
curious forms of diction, which have no intelligible meaning what-
ever, is not a subject for children to play with; it is a subject for
psychologists to go mad over.*

The Hunting of the Snark is a poem over which an unstable,
sensitive soul might very well go mad. There is even a touch of
madness in the reverse, looking-glass procedure by which it was
written. The time was 1874. The Reverend Charles Lutwidge
Dodgson, that shy and fastidious bachelor who taught mathe-
matics at Christ Church, Oxford, was then 42 and something of a
celebrity. He had written two masterpieces that were to immor-
talize his child friend, Alice Liddell, and he had published *Phantas-*

* 'The Library of the Nursery', *Lunacy and Letters*, 1958.

magoria, a small book of (mostly dull) nonsense poems. On the afternoon of 18 July, in Guildford, the town in Surrey where his sisters lived, Carroll went out for a stroll. This is how he tells the story:

I was walking on a hillside, alone, one bright summer day, when suddenly there came into my head one line of verse – one solitary line – 'For the Snark *was* a Boojum, you see.' I knew not what it meant, then: I know not what it means, now; but I wrote it down: and, sometime afterwards, the rest of the stanza occurred to me, that being its last line: and so by degrees, at odd moments during the next year or two, the rest of the poem pieced itself together, that being its last stanza.*

The poem is first mentioned in Carroll's diary in an entry on 23 November 1874: 'Ruskin came, by my request, for a talk about the pictures Holiday is doing for the "Boojum" – one (the scene on board) has been cut on wood. He much disheartened me by holding out no hopes that Holiday would be able to illustrate a book satisfactorily.'

Henry Holiday was a prominent London painter and sculptor, later a celebrated designer of stained-glass windows. His auto-biography, *Reminiscences of My Life*, reproduces a number of his murals: mostly historical scenes, painted in a classical manner and swarming with nudes and Grecian-robed figures. His stained-glass windows were shipped to churches all over the globe, including dozens in the United States, some in large cities, some in towns as small as Wappingers Falls, New York, and Thermopolis, Wyoming. His best works, he thought, were the windows – in particular the two huge scenes of the Crucifixion and the Ascension – that he designed and cast for The Church of the Holy Trinity at 316 East Eighty-eighth Street in Manhattan. (They are worth a visit. I sometimes wonder how many of the parishioners, worshipping on Sunday morning, are aware of the fact that these pious patterns of coloured glass were designed by the illustrator of *The Hunting of*

* 'Alice on the Stage', *The Theatre*, April 1887.

the Snark.) If anyone had suggested to Holiday that he might be remembered chiefly for his pictures in the *Snark*, or that his autobiography would be collected mainly because of its references to Carroll, he would have been incredulous; as incredulous as Dean Henry George Liddell's official biographer if someone had suggested that among the academic associates of Alice's father, the one destined for the greatest fame was a man nowhere mentioned in the biography!

Carroll first met Holiday in 1870 when the artist visited Oxford to paint a frieze in one of the college chapels. On 15 January 1874 Carroll mentions in his diary that Holiday had given him a series of exquisite drawings of nude children and that he (Carroll) planned to copy them in photographs from life. 'Told Holiday of an idea his drawings suggested to me, that he might illustrate a child's book for me. If *only* he can draw grotesques, it would be all I should desire – the grace and beauty of his pictures would quite rival Tenniel, I think.'

How well the academician Holiday succeeded in producing grotesques for the *Snark* (it is the only work of Carroll's that he illustrated) is open to debate. Ruskin was certainly right in thinking him inferior to Tenniel. His drawings are, of course, thoroughly realistic except for the oversize heads and the slightly surrealist quality that derives less from the artist's imagination than from the fact that he was illustrating a surrealist poem.

In his article on 'The Snark's Significance', Holiday writes that after Carroll had completed three fits of his poem, he

asked if I would design three illustrations to them, explaining that the composition would some day be introduced in a book he was contemplating; but as this latter would certainly not be ready for a considerable time, he thought of printing the poem for private circulation in the first instance. While I was making sketches for these illustrations, he sent me a fourth 'fit', asking for another drawing; shortly after came a fifth 'fit', with a similar request, and this was followed by a sixth, seventh, and eighth. His mind not being occupied with any other book at the time, this theme seemed continually to be suggesting new developments; and having extended the 'agony' thus far beyond his original intentions, Mr Dodgson decided to publish it at once as an independent work, without waiting for *Sylvie and Bruno*, of which it was to have formed a feature.

I rather regretted the extension [Holiday continues] as it seemed to me to involve a disproportion between the scale of the work and its substance; and I doubted if the expansion were not greater than so slight a structure would bear. The 'Walrus and Carpenter' appeared to be happier in its proportions, and it mattered little whether or not it could establish a claim to be classified among literary vertebrata. However, on re-reading the *Snark* now I feel it to be unquestionably funny throughout, and I cannot wish any part cut out; so I suppose my fears were unfounded.

One of Holiday's sketches was never used. This is how he explains it:

In our correspondence about the illustrations, the coherence and consistency of the nonsense on its own nonsensical understanding often became prominent. One of the first three I had to do was the disappearance of the Baker, and I not unnaturally invented a Boojum. Mr Dodgson wrote that it was a delightful monster, but that it was inadmissible. All his descriptions of the Boojum were quite unimaginable, and he wanted the creature to remain so. I assented, of course, though reluctant to dismiss what I am still confident is an accurate representation. I hope that some future Darwin, in a new *Beagle*, will find the beast, or its remains; if he does, I know he will confirm my drawing.*

Carroll records in his diary on 25 October 1875 that he has the sudden notion of publishing the *Snark* as a Christmas poem. Four days later this plan collapses when he hears from Macmillan that

* This suppressed drawing of the Boojum is reproduced opposite. It was first published in 1932 (the centennial of Carroll's birth) in the *Listener*, 29 June, page 922, and the *Illustrated London News*, 9 July, page 48. Harold Hartley, in an article on 'Lewis Carroll and His Artists and Engravers' in the *Lewis Carroll Centenary Exhibition Catalogue*, edited by Falconer Madan (London: Bumpus Ltd, 1932), writes that he owns the original, having purchased it directly from Holiday.

The 'suppressed' Boojum

it will take at least three months to complete the wood engravings. On 5 November he mentions sending to Macmillan the text of three fits. The following day he writes four more stanzas, 'completing the poem'. 7 November he sends his 'finished' manuscript to Macmillan, but in January of the following year we find him still working on new fits and adding more stanzas to old ones.

The book was finally published in late March 1876, shortly before Easter. This gave Carroll an excuse for inserting into the volume a small pamphlet (later sold separately) entitled 'An Easter Greeting'. He realized that the religious sentiments in this greeting were out of keeping with the ballad, but he notes in his diary that he did not 'like to lose the opportunity of saying a few serious words to (perhaps) 20,000 children'. In addition, he may have had a vague, uncomfortable feeling that the gloom and pessimism of his poem needed to be balanced by a reference to the Easter message of hope.

On 29 March Carroll records that he spent six hours at Macmillan inscribing some eighty presentation copies of his book. Many of these inscriptions were acrostic verses on the names of little girls to whom the books were sent. The following two have often been reprinted:

'ARE you deaf, Father William?' the young man said,
'Did you hear what I told you just now?
'Excuse me for shouting! Don't waggle your head
'Like a blundering, sleepy old cow!
'A little maid dwelling in Wallington Town,
'Is my friend, so I beg to remark:
'Do you think she'd be pleased if a book were sent down
'Entitled "The Hunt of the Snark"?'

'Pack it up in brown paper!' the old man cried,
'And seal it with olive-and-dove.
'I command you to do it!' he added with pride,
'Nor forget, my good fellow, to send her beside
'Easter Greetings, and give her my love.'

MAIDEN, though thy heart may quail
And thy quivering lip grow pale,
Read the Bellman's tragic tale!

Is it life of which it tells?
Of a pulse that sinks and swells
Never lacking chime of bells?

Bells of sorrow, bells of cheer,
Easter, Christmas, glad New Year,
Still they sound, afar, anear.

So may Life's sweet bells for thee,
In the summers yet to be,
Evermore make melody!

Is it life of which it tells? If so, what aspect of life is being told? We know that the *Snark* describes 'with infinite humor the impossible voyage of an improbable crew to find an inconceivable creature', as Sidney Williams and Falconer Madan put it in their *Handbook of the Literature of the Rev. C. L. Dodgson*. But is that *all* it describes?

Every serious reader of the *Snark* has pondered this question, and many have tried to answer it. Carroll himself was, of course, asked it repeatedly. On the record, he answered it five times.

1. 'Periodically I have received courteous letters from strangers,' Carroll wrote in 'Alice on the Stage', 'begging to know whether *The Hunting of the Snark* is an allegory, or contains some hidden moral, or is a political satire: and for all such questions I have but one answer, "*I don't know!*" '

2. In 1876 he wrote to a child friend: 'When you have read the *Snark*, I hope you will write me a little note and tell me how you like it, and if you can *quite* understand it. Some children are puzzled with it. Of course you know what a Snark is? If you do, please tell *me*: for I haven't an idea what it is like. And tell me which of the pictures you like best.'

3. This from a letter written in 1880 to a not-so-little girl of nineteen: 'I have a letter from you ... asking me "Why don't you explain the *Snark*?", a question I ought to have answered long ago. Let me answer it now – "because I can't". Are you able to explain things which you don't yourself understand?'

4. In 1896, twenty years after the ballad was published, he is still struggling with the question.

As to the meaning of the *Snark*? [he writes in a long letter to a group of children] I'm very much afraid I didn't mean anything but nonsense! Still, you know, words mean more than we mean to express when we use them: so a whole book ought to mean a great deal more than the writer meant. So, whatever good meanings are in the book, I'm very glad to accept as the meaning of the book. The best that I've seen is by a lady (she published it in a letter to a newspaper) – that the whole book is an allegory on the search after happiness. I think this fits beautifully in many ways – particularly about the bathing-machines: when the people get weary of life, and can't find happiness in town or in books, then they rush off to the seaside to see what bathing-machines will do for them.

5. Carroll's last comment on the *Snark* was in a letter written in 1897, a year before his death:

In answer to your question, 'What did you mean the Snark was?' will you tell your friend that I meant that the Snark was a *Boojum*. I trust that she and you will now feel quite satisfied and happy.

To the best of my recollection, I had no other meaning in my mind, when I wrote it: but people have since tried to find the meanings in it. The one I like best (which I think is partly my own) is that it may be taken as an allegory for the pursuit of happiness. The characteristic 'ambition' works well into this theory – and also its fondness for bathing-machines, as indicating that the pursuer of happiness, when he has exhausted all other devices, betakes himself, as a last and desperate resource, to some such wretched watering-place as East-bourne, and hopes to find, in the tedious and depressing society of the daughters of mistresses of boarding-schools, the happiness he has failed to find elsewhere. . . .

There is no reason to suppose that Carroll was in the slightest degree evasive in denying that he had intended his poem to mean anything at all. But, as he himself pointed out, words can mean much more than a writer intends. They can express meanings buried so deep in an author's mind that he himself is not aware of them, and they can acquire meanings entirely by accident. Nonsense writing is a peculiarly rich medium for both types of 'unintended' meaning.

'I can remember a clever undergraduate at Oxford,' writes Holiday in 'The Snark's Significance', 'who knew the *Snark* by heart, telling me that on all sorts of occasions, in all the daily incidents of life, some line from the poem was sure to occur to him that exactly fitted. Most people will have noticed this peculiarity of Lewis Carroll's writing.' When a Carrollian nonsense line suggests one of these neat metaphorical applications, who can say, particularly in the case of the *Snark*, whether the fit is fortuitous or whether it derives from a level below the Fit – that dark, unconscious substratum of intent that underlies all great creative acts?

Many attempts have been made to force the whole of the *Snark* into one overall metaphorical pattern. A writer with the initials M.H.T., in a note appended to Holiday's article on the ballad's significance, argues that the Snark represents material wealth. 'I am always lost in astonishment,' he says, 'at the people who think it can be anything else. Observe the things with which its capture was attempted. Why, the mere mention of railway shares and soap is sufficient of itself to establish my thesis.' The Boojum, according to this writer, is that type of unexpected good fortune that lifts a man 'into a sphere in which he is miserable, and makes his wife cut the greengrocer's lady'.

A second note to Holiday's article, this one signed St. J.E.C.H., takes the position that the poem is a satire on the craving for social advancement; the tragedy of the person who tries to climb into society but never gets higher on the ladder than the local Browning club.

Two events that took place at the time Carroll's ballad was being written gave rise to two popular theories about the poem. One event was the famous trial of the Tichborne claimant, discussed in Note 49. The other was an arctic expedition on two steamships, the *Alert* and *Discovery*, that set out from Portsmouth in 1875, returning in the fall of 1876. The expedition was much in the news before and after the publication of the *Snark*, and many readers apparently supposed that the ballad was a satire on an arctic voyage, the Snark a symbol of the North Pole. There is little to recommend this theory, although the polar expedition, like the Tichborne case, undoubtedly added to the topical interest of the poem.

A theory closely related to the material-wealth theory of M.H.T. was proposed in 1911 by Devereux Court in an article in the *Cornhill Magazine*. Court thought that the poem satirized an unsound business venture. The ship's company is the business company. The vessel has been 'floated'. The men on board are the men on the company's board of directors, all of them speculators fond of 'quotations'. The Bellman is the chairman of the board, the Boots the secretary. The Snark is a land shark who brings about the company's downfall.

The latest variant of this interpretation was advanced in the early thirties by Dean Wallace B. Donham of the Harvard School of Business Administration. His views are defended at length in an article, 'Finding of the Snark', by Arthur Ruhl, in the *Saturday Review of Literature*, 18 March 1933. Dean Donham's opinion is that the *Snark* is a satire on business in general, the Boojum a symbol of a business slump, and the whole thing a tragedy about the business cycle. In 1933 the United States was of course in the midst of the great depression. The poem's allegorical level is worked out with considerable ingenuity: the Boots is unskilled labour, the Beaver is a textile worker, the Baker a small businessman in a luxury trade, the Billiard-marker a speculator, the hyenas are stockbrokers, the bear is a stock market bear, the Jubjub is Disraeli, and so on. The Bandersnatch, who keeps snatching at the Banker in Fit 7, is the Bank of England, repeatedly raising its interest rate in the wild optimism that preceded the panic of 1875. It was Dean Donham's belief that 'no single quatrain in the *Snark* goes contra to the interpretation', but the reader will have to consult Ruhl's article for a fuller defence of that statement.

The most elaborate and witty of all Snark theories is the tongue-in-cheek concoction of the philosopher Ferdinand Canning Scott Schiller. Schiller is almost forgotten today, but at the turn of the century he was recognized, along with William James and John Dewey, as one of the three principal leaders of the pragmatic movement. Schiller had a zest for logical paradoxes, practical jokes, and outrageous puns. (He would have made a sterling member of the Snark hunting crew, under the name of the Bachelor; he managed to avoid marrying until he was 71.) In 1901, when he was teaching philosophy at Oxford, he persuaded the editors of *Mind*, a philosophical journal, to bring out a parody issue. Schiller's 'Commentary on the Snark', for which he used the pseudonym of Snarkophilus Snobbs, is the highlight of this issue. It interprets Carroll's ballad as a satire on the Hegelian philosopher's search for the Absolute. The full text of this commentary will be found in the appendix of this book, so I shall say no more about it here.

Is there more to be said about the *Snark*? Yes, there is yet another way of looking at the poem, an existentialist way if you will, that for several reasons is singularly appropriate to our time.

The key to this interpretation is in the last five stanzas of Fit 3. The Baker's uncle, perhaps on his deathbed, has just informed the Baker that if the Snark he confronts turns out to be a Boojum, he will 'softly and suddenly vanish away, and never be met with again!' In the next four stanzas the Baker describes his emotional reaction to this solemn warning. In keeping with the Bellman's rule-of-three, he says it three times to underscore the truth of what he is saying. He is in a state of acute existential nausea.

'It is this, it is this that oppresses my soul,
  When I think of my uncle's last words:
And my heart is like nothing so much as a bowl
  Brimming over with quivering curds!'

This state of existential anxiety, as the existential analysts like to call it (earlier ages called it simply the fear of death), is of course a thoroughly normal emotion. But, for one reason or another, both individuals and cultures vary widely in the degree to which they suppress this emotion. At the moment, at least in England and the United States, death as a natural process has become almost unmentionable. As Geoffrey Gorer puts it in his article on 'The Pornography of Death',* one of the peculiar features of our time is that while violent death, and the possibility of violent death, has greatly increased, and while it plays an 'ever-growing part in the fantasies offered to mass audiences – detective stories, thrillers, Westerns, war stories, spy stories, science fiction, and eventually horror comics', talk about natural death has become 'more and more smothered in prudery'. It is the great conversation stopper of parlour discourse.

Lewis Carroll lived in a different age, an age in which death was domesticated and sentimentalized, an age in which readers were able to weep real tears over the passing of Dickens's Little Nell. Carroll thought a great deal about death and, I am persuaded, about the possibility of his own nonexistence. Jokes about death abound in his writings, even in the *Alice* books. His rejection of the doctrine of eternal punishment was his one major departure from Protestant orthodoxy. In the introduction to his book *Pillow Problems* he speaks of the value of mental work at night in keeping one's mind free of unholy thoughts. 'There are sceptical thoughts, which seem for the moment to uproot the firmest faith; there are blasphemous thoughts, which dart unbidden into the most reverent souls; there are unholy thoughts, which torture with their hateful presence, the fancy that would fain be pure.'

* *Encounter*, October 1955.

I believe that Carroll is describing here a state of existential dread. I think it is what he had in mind, perhaps not consciously, when he has the Baker say:

> 'I engage with the Snark – every night after dark –
>   In a dreamy delirious fight:
> I serve it with greens in those shadowy scenes,
>   And I use it for striking a light.'

Its use for striking a light – the light of faith – is the central theme of Miguel de Unamuno's great existential work, *The Tragic Sense of Life*. Dozens of books have been written in the past decade or two about the existentialist movement, but for some impenetrable reason most of them do not even mention Unamuno, the Spanish poet, novelist and philosopher (he died in 1936) whose outlook is certainly closer to Kierkegaard's than that of many philosophers who wear the existentialist label. The Baker's remarks about his uncle's last words are a metaphorical compression of scores of passages that can be found in Unamuno's writings. Here is a moving example from his commentary on *Don Quixote*:

. . . one of those moments when the soul is blown about by a sudden gust from the wings of the angel of mystery. A moment of anguish. For there are times when, unsuspecting, we are suddenly seized, we know not how nor whence, by a vivid sense of our mortality, which takes us without warning and quite unprepared. When most absorbed in the cares and duties of life, or engrossed and self-forgetful on some festal occasion or engaged in a pleasant chat, suddenly it seems that death is fluttering over me. Not death, something worse, a sensation of annihilation, a supreme anguish. And this anguish, tearing us violently from our perception of appearances, with a single stunning swoop, dashes us away – to recover into an awareness of the substance of things.

All creation is something we are some day to lose, and is some day to lose us. For what else is it to vanish from the world but the world vanishing from us? Can you conceive of yourself as not existing? Try it. Concentrate your imagination on it. Fancy yourself without vision,

27

hearing, the sense of touch, the ability to perceive anything. Try it. Perhaps you will evoke and bring upon yourself that anguish which visits us when least expected; perhaps you will feel the hangman's knot choking off your soul's breath. Like the woodpecker in the oak-tree, an agony is busily pecking at our hearts, to make its nest there.

It is this agony, the agony of anticipating one's loss of being, that pecks at the heart of Carroll's poem. Did he realize that B, the dominant letter of his ballad, is a symbol of 'be'? I sometimes think he did. At any rate, the letter sounds through the poem like a continuous drum beat, starting softly with the introduction of the Bellman, the Boots, and the others, then growing more and more insistent until, in a final thunderclap, it becomes the Boojum.

The *Snark* is a poem about being and non-being, an existential poem, a poem of existential agony. The Bellman's map is the map that charts the course of humanity; blank because we possess no information about where we are or whither we drift. The ship's bowsprit gets mixed with its rudder and when we think we sail west we sail east. The Snark is, in Paul Tillich's fashionable phrase, every man's ultimate concern. This is the great search motif of the poem, the quest for an ultimate good. But this motif is submerged in a stronger motif, the dread, the agonizing dread, of ultimate failure. The Boojum is more than death. It is the end of all searching. It is final, absolute extinction. In a literal sense, Carroll's Boojum means nothing at all. It is the void, the great blank emptiness out of which we miraculously emerged; by which we will ultimately be devoured; through which the absurd galaxies spiral and drift endlessly on their nonsense voyages from nowhere to nowhere.

Perhaps you are a naturalist and humanist, or a Sartrean existentialist. You believe passionately in working for a better world, and although you know that you will not be around to enjoy it, you take a kind of comfort – poor substitute that it is! – from the fact that future generations, perhaps even your own children, may reap the rewards of your labours. But what if they won't? Atomic energy is a Snark that comes in various shapes and sizes. A certain number of intercontinental guided missiles – the U.S. Air Force has one it calls the Snark – with thermonuclear warheads can glide gently down on the just and unjust, and the whole of humanity may never be met with again.

For the Snark was a. . . .

We are poised now on the brink of discovering the unsuspected meaning that Carroll's poem acquired in 1942 when Enrico Fermi and his associates (working, appropriately, in a former 'squash' court) obtained the first sustained nuclear chain reaction.

Consider for a moment that remarkable four-letter word *bomb*. It begins and ends with *b*. The second *b* is silent; the final silence. B for birth, non-*b* for Nothing. Between the two *b*'s (to be or not to be) is *Om*, Hindu symbol for the nature of Brahman, the Absolute, the god behind the lesser gods whose tasks are to create, preserve, and destroy all that is.

'I believe it [the atom bomb] is the greatest of all American inventions,' declared H. L. Mencken, 'and one of the imperishable glories of Christianity. It surpasses the burning of heretics on all counts, but especially on the count that it has given the world an entirely new disease, to wit, galloping carcinoma.'* This disease advanced to a new stage in August 1961, when Khrushchev announced that the Soviet Union would unilaterally resume nuclear testing, perhaps build a 100-megaton bomb. A political cartoon in the *Boston Traveler* showed Khrushchev sticking his head around a corner, a cloud mushrooming from his mouth and bearing the single word 'BOO'. No Snarxist need be told 'the word he was trying to say'.

A bookish pastime, recommended for whiling away the hours left to us in these tropical climes of cancer, is that of searching odd corners of literature for passages unintentionally prophetic of the Bomb. Here, for example, is Vincent Starrett's poem 'Portent'.†

* As quoted in *Life*, 5 August 1946.
† From *Flame and Dust*, 1924. Starrett's book title is another portent!

'Heavy, heavy – over thy head –'
  Hear them call in the room below!
Now they patter with gruesome tread,
  Now they riot with laugh and blow.
  Tchk! What a pity that they must grow!
'Heavy, heavy – over thy head –'

'Heavy, heavy – over thy head –'
  Winds are bleak as they coil and blow.
Once the sky was a golden red;
  Once *I* played in that room below.
  Sometimes I think that children know!
'Heavy, heavy – over thy head –'

Paul Goodman's novel, *The Grand Piano* (1941), closes with its
hero, Horatio Alger, wiring an explosive to the piano key of B
flat (Carroll's B again!) just below the centre of the keyboard.
The idea is to play a composition in which the tones cluster around
the death note, never touching it, but always calling for it as a
resolution.

This is, of course, precisely the wild, demonic music that the
U.S. and the U.S.S.R. are now playing, and in which other, less
skilful musicians will soon be joining. It is this background music
that gives to Lewis Carroll's poem, when it is read today, a new
dimension of anxiety. The Baker is Man himself, on the Brink,
erect, sublime, wagging his head like an idiot, cackling with
laughter and glee.

Suddenly that startled, choked-off cry, 'It's a Boo —'

Then silence. . . .

Perhaps otherwise. Perhaps the Bomb will prove to be not a
Boojum but only a harmless variety of Snark. The human race
will continue to creep onward and upward, stretching out its
hands, as H. G. Wells liked to say, to the stars. Take comfort from
such happy thoughts, you who can. The Boojum remains. Like
T. S. Eliot's eternal Footman, it snickers at the coat tails of every
member of humanity's motley crew.

> Twilight and evening bell,
> And after that the Snark!

These lines could serve as a caption for the poem's final illustration. Beyond the craggy precipice, in the shadows of a terrible twilight, a man of flesh and bone is vanishing. Send not to know, dear reader, for whom the Bellman's bell tolls.

The Hunting of the Snark

LEWIS CARROLL

With notes by Martin Gardner

Inscribed to a dear Child:
in memory of golden summer hours
*and whispers of a summer sea*1*

GIRT with a boyish garb for boyish task,
    Eager she wields her spade: yet loves as well
Rest on a friendly knee, intent to ask
    The tale he loves to tell.2*

Rude spirits of the seething outer strife,
    Unmeet to read her pure and simple spright,
Deem, if you list, such hours a waste of life
    Empty of all delight!

Chat on, sweet Maid, and rescue from annoy
    Hearts that by wiser talk are unbeguiled.
Ah, happy he who owns that tenderest joy,
    The heart-love of a child!

Away, fond thoughts, and vex my soul no more!
    Work claims my wakeful nights, my busy days –
Albeit bright memories of that sunlit shore
    Yet haunt my dreaming gaze!

---

1. Of the many acrostics that Lewis Carroll wrote for his child friends, this is perhaps the most ingenious. Not only do the initial letters of the lines spell Gertrude Chataway, but her name is also indicated by the first words of each stanza: *Girt, Rude, Chat, Away.*

* Notes to Lewis Carroll's dedication and prefatory poem begin on page 36.

Carroll made friends with hundreds of little girls, but there were several of whom he was particularly fond and who received more than his usual attention. The first and most intense of these special friendships was, of course, with Alice Liddell, the original of his fictional Alice. Gertrude was the second. He first met her in 1875 on the beach at Sandown, a small bathing resort town on the Isle of Wight. She was in the company of her parents – her father was a clergyman – and three sisters. Gertrude was then almost eight. This is how she later recalled the occasion (from *The Life and Letters of Lewis Carroll*, by Stuart Collingwood):

I first met Mr Lewis Carroll on the sea-shore at Sandown in the Isle of Wight, in the summer of 1875, when I was quite a little child.

We had all been taken there for change of air, and next door there was an old gentleman – to me at any rate he seemed old – who interested me immensely. He would come on to his balcony, which joined ours, sniffing the sea-air with his head thrown back, and would walk right down the steps on to the beach with his chin in air, drinking in the fresh breezes as if he could never have enough. I do not know why this excited such keen curiosity on my part, but I remember well that whenever I heard his footstep I flew out to see him coming, and when one day he spoke to me my joy was complete.

Thus we made friends, and in a very little while I was as familiar with the interior of his lodgings as with our own.

I had the usual child's love for fairy-tales and marvels, and his power of telling stories naturally fascinated me. We used to sit for hours on the wooden steps which led from our garden on to the beach, whilst he told the most lovely tales that could possibly be imagined, often illustrating the exciting situations with a pencil as he went along.

One thing that made his stories particularly charming to a child was that he often took his cue from her remarks – a question would set him off on quite a new trail of ideas, so that one felt that one had somehow helped to make the story, and it seemed a personal possession. It was the most lovely nonsense conceivable, and I naturally revelled in it. His vivid imagination would fly from one subject to another, and was never tied down in any way by the probabilities of life.

To *me* it was of course all perfect, but it is astonishing that *he* never seemed either tired or to want other society. I spoke to him once of this since I have been grown up, and he told me it was the greatest pleasure he could have to converse freely with a child, and feel the depths of her mind.

He used to write to me and I to him after that summer, and the friendship, thus begun, lasted. His letters were one of the greatest joys of my childhood.

I don't think that he ever really understood that we, whom he had known as children, could not always remain such. I stayed with him only a few years ago, at Eastbourne, and felt for the time that I was once more a child. He never appeared to realize that I had grown up, except when I reminded him of the fact and then he only said, 'Never mind: you will always be a child to me, even when your hair is grey.'

A pencil sketch by Carroll, of Gertrude Chataway at the seaside

A pencil sketch that Carroll made of Gertrude, wearing her 'boyish garb', is reproduced opposite page 107 in Evelyn Hatch's *Selection from the Letters of Lewis Carroll to His Child-friends* (and is also reproduced above). Some of Carroll's letters to Gertrude will be found in that volume, others in Collingwood's biography. Carroll's friendships with little girls usually cooled when they reached adolescence, but Gertrude was an exception. When she was 25 he wrote her an affectionate letter, recalling 'like a dream of fifty years ago' the 'little bare-legged girl in a sailor's jersey, who used to run up into my lodgings by the sea'. In his diary Carroll notes on 19 September 1893 that Gertrude (then almost 27) arrived for a visit at his lodging in Eastbourne. The next entry, four days later, is 'Gertrude left. It has been a really delightful visit.'

It was this visit, Roger Green discloses in his commentary on the diary, that prompted a letter from Carroll's sister, raising the question of whether it was proper for him to permit young ladies, unescorted, to visit him at the seaside. Carroll's reply, quoted by Green, is characteristic:

I think all you say about my girl-guests is most kind and sisterly. . . . But I don't think it is at all advisable to enter into any controversy about it. There is no reasonable probability that it would modify the views either of you or of me. I will say a few words to explain my views: but I have no wish whatever to have 'the last word', so please say anything you like afterwards.

You and your husband have, I think, been very fortunate to know so little, by experience, in your own case, or in that of your friends, of the wicked reck-lessness with which people repeat things to the disadvantage of others, without a thought as to whether they have grounds for asserting what they say. I have met with a good deal of utter mis-representation of that kind. And another result of my experience is that the opinion of 'people' in general is absolutely worthless as a test of right and wrong. The only two tests I now apply to such a question as having some particular girl-friend as a guest are, first, my own conscience, to settle whether I feel it to be entirely innocent and right, in the sight of God: secondly, the parents of my friend, to settle whether I have their *full* approval of

what I do. You need not be shocked at my being spoken against. *Any*body, who is spoken about at all, is *sure* to be spoken against by *some*body: and any action, however innocent in itself, is liable, and not at all unlikely, to be blamed by *somebody*. If you limit your actions in life to things that *nobody* can possibly find fault with, you will not do much. . . .

It is interesting to note in Carroll's diary (though it may be sheer coincidence) that nine days before Gertrude arrived on her visit, Carroll preached a sermon in Eastbourne on the text 'Lead us not into temptation.'

When Carroll completed his acrostic poem to Gertrude, about a month after first meeting her, he mailed a copy to Mrs Chataway with a request for permission to print it some day. Evidently she did not notice the concealed name because after hearing from her, Carroll wrote again to call her attention to the double acrostic and to ask if this made any difference in the permission she had given. 'If I print them,' he wrote, 'I shan't tell anyone it is an acrostic — but someone will be sure to find it out before long.'

Ten days later he wrote again to tell Gertrude's mother of his plans to use the poem as a dedication in his forthcoming book, *The Hunting of the Snark*. 'The scene is laid,' he writes, 'in an island frequented by the Jubjub and Bandersnatch – no doubt the very island in which the Jabberwock was slain.'

2. In Carroll's first version of this poem, as he sent it to Gertrude's mother for approval (see *A Selection from the Letters of Lewis Carroll to His Child-friends*, page 107), the last two lines of the first stanza read:

Rest on a friendly knee, the tale to ask
      That he delights to tell.

A third version of the poem, with minor alterations, appears as the inscription of Carroll's book of poems, *Rhyme? and Reason?*

PREFACE

Lewis Carroll

IF – and the thing is wildly possible – the charge of writing non-sense were ever brought against the author of this brief but instructive poem, it would be based, I feel convinced, on the line,

'Then the bowsprit got mixed with the rudder sometimes.'

In view of this painful possibility, I will not (as I might) appeal indignantly to my other writings as a proof that I am incapable of such a deed: I will not (as I might) point to the strong moral purpose of this poem itself, to the arithmetical principles so cautiously inculcated in it, or to its noble teachings in Natural History - I will take the more prosaic course of simply explaining how it happened.

The Bellman, who was almost morbidly sensitive about appearances, used to have the bowsprit unshipped once or twice a week to be revarnished, and it more than once happened, when the time came for replacing it, that no one on board could remember which end of the ship it belonged to. They knew it was not of the slightest use to appeal to the Bellman about it – he would only refer to his Naval Code, and read out in pathetic tones Admiralty Instructions which none of them had ever been able to understand – so it generally ended in its being fastened on, anyhow, across the rudder. The helmsman * used to stand by with tears in his eyes: *he* knew it was all wrong, but alas! Rule 42 of the Code, '*No one shall speak to the Man at the Helm,*' had been completed by the Bellman himself with the words '*and the Man at the Helm shall*

---

* This office was usually undertaken by the Boots, who found in it a refuge from the Baker's constant complaints about the insufficient blacking of his three pair of boots.

speak to no one'. So remonstrance was impossible, and no steering could be done till the next varnishing day. During these bewildering intervals the ship usually sailed backwards.

As this poem is to some extent connected with the lay of the Jabberwock, let me take this opportunity of answering a question that has often been asked me, how to pronounce 'slithy toves'. The 'i' in 'slithy' is long, as in 'writhe'; and 'toves' is pronounced so as to rhyme with 'groves'. Again, the first 'o' in 'borogoves' is pronounced like the 'o' in 'borrow'. I have heard people try to give it the sound of the 'o' in 'worry'. Such is Human Perversity.

This also seems a fitting occasion to notice the other hard words in that poem. Humpty-Dumpty's theory, of two meanings packed into one word like a portmanteau, seems to me the right explanation for all.

For instance, take the two words 'fuming' and 'furious'. Make up your mind that you will say both words, but leave it unsettled which you will say first. Now open your mouth and speak. If your thoughts incline ever so little towards 'fuming', you will say 'fuming-furious'; if they turn, by even a hair's breadth, towards 'furious', you will say 'furious-fuming'; but if you have that rarest of gifts, a perfectly balanced mind, you will say 'frumious'.

Supposing that, when Pistol uttered the well-known words –

'Under which king, Bezonian? Speak or die!'

Justice Shallow had felt certain that it was either William or Richard, but had not been able to settle which, so that he could not possibly say either name before the other, can it be doubted that, rather than die, he would have gasped out 'Rilchiam!'

THE HUNTING OF THE SNARK

An Agony, in Eight Fits [3]

3. *Agony* is here used in the old sense of a struggle that involves great anguish, bodily pain, or death. Carroll also may have had in mind the 'woeful agony' that periodically seizes Coleridge's Ancient Mariner, forcing him to tell to strangers his 'ghastly tale'.

Fit has the double meaning of a convulsion and a canto. *The Oxford English Dictionary* quotes Samuel Johnson: 'A long ballad in many fits', and Lord Byron: 'one fytte of Harold's pilgrimage'. Phyllis Green-acre, in her psychoanalytical study of Carroll (*Swift and Carroll*, 1955), thinks there is some connexion between the fact that Carroll's poem has eight fits and Carroll had eight younger siblings.

Carroll had once before punned on the word 'fit'. In the first *Alice* book, during the trial of the Knave of Hearts, the King quotes the poetic line, 'before she had this fit'. 'You never had fits, my dear, I think?' he asks his wife. When she replies 'Never!' the King says, 'Then the words don't *fit* you.' This produces dead silence in the courtroom.

Supporting each man on the top of the tide

Fit the First

THE LANDING

'JUST the place for a Snark!'[4] the Bellman[5] cried,
  As he landed his crew with care;
Supporting each man on the top of the tide
  By a finger entwined in his hair.[6]

4. Beatrice Hatch, in her article 'Lewis Carroll' (the *Strand Magazine*, April 1898, pages 413–23), says that Carroll once told her that *Snark* was a portmanteau word for *snail* and *shark*; but 'one suspects,' writes Phyllis Greenacre, 'that snake has crept into this portmanteau.' Stephen Barr, a correspondent in Woodstock, N.Y., suggests *snarl* and *bark* as another pair of meanings that may be packed together here.

5. *Bellman* is another word for a town crier. The Bellman is, of course, the captain of the ship and the man who organized the Snark hunt. On early ships a bell would be struck every half hour to indicate the number of half hours that had elapsed in each four-hour watch, so perhaps this is one of the Bellman's chores. Perhaps, also, there is a connexion between the agony's eight fits and the fact that eight bells marked the end of a watch.

Contemporary readers fancied a resemblance to Tennyson in Holiday's pictures of the Bellman. The Bellman appears, whole or in part, in every illustration except the one of the Butcher sharpening his hatchet.

6. The crew member shown supported by his hair in Holiday's illustration for this stanza is the Banker. He is carrying a telescope (see Fit 5, Note 40). The word *Swain* in the lower right corner is the surname of Joseph Swain, the man who made the wood engravings from Holiday's original drawings.

'Just the place for a Snark! I have said it twice:
That alone should encourage the crew.
Just the place for a Snark! I have said it thrice:
What I tell you three times is true.'[7]

7. The Bellman's rule-of-three is invoked later (Fit 5) to establish the presence of the Jubjub, though the Beaver has considerable difficulty making sure that three statements have in fact occurred. Norbert Wiener, in his book *Cybernetics*, points out that answers given by a computer are often checked by asking the computer to solve the same problem several times, or by giving the problem to several different computers. Wiener speculates on whether the human brain contains a similar checking mechanism:

We can hardly expect that any important message is entrusted for transmission to a single neuron, nor that any important operation is entrusted to a single neuronal mechanism. Like the computing machine, the brain probably works on a variant of the famous principle expounded by Lewis Carroll in *The Hunting of the Snark*: 'What I tell you three times is true.'

The rule-of-three plays a central role in the plot of a bizarre science fiction story, 'Chaos, Co-ordinated', by John MacDougal (pseudonym of Robert Lowndes and James Blish). The earth is at war with a distant galaxy, where the various races are coordinated by a gigantic computer. An earthman manages to disguise

The Hunting of the Snark as an 'observational report' and feed it to the giant brain. The brain accepts literally the order 'What I tell you three times is true.' All it had been told once or twice in the past is regarded as unverified, and new observational reports are not accepted because they are made only once. As a result the entire galaxy becomes, so to speak, snarked. The machine issues blank star maps, distributes bells to spaceship captains, stocks medical chests with muffins, ice, mustard and cress, jam, two volumes of proverbs, and a recording of riddles beginning with 'Why is a raven like a writing desk?' (See Fit 3, Stanza 1.) The story appeared in *Astounding Science Fiction*, October 1946.

The American writer Edith Wharton was fond of the *Snark* when she was a little girl. In her autobiography, *A Backward Glance* (1934), pages 311–12, she tells of a lunch with President Theodore Roosevelt, whom she had known since her childhood. 'Well,' he said, 'I *am* glad to welcome to the White House someone to whom I can quote *The Hunting of the Snark* without being asked what I mean! ... Would you believe it, no one in

The crew was complete: it included a Boots – [8]
A maker of Bonnets and Hoods –
A Barrister, brought to arrange their disputes –
And a Broker, [9] to value their goods.

A Billiard-marker, [10] whose skill was immense,
Might perhaps have won more than his share –
But a Banker, engaged at enormous expense,
Had the whole of their cash in his care.

the administration has ever heard of Alice, much less of the Snark, and the other day, when I said to the Secretary of Navy: "Mr Secretary, *What I say three times is true*", he did not recognize the allusion, and answered with an aggrieved air: "Mr President, it would never for a moment have occurred to me to impugn your veracity"!'

8. A 'boots' is a servant at a hotel or inn, assigned to such low tasks as the shining of boots and shoes. No one knows what the Boots looks like; he is the one crew member who does not appear in any of Holiday's pictures.

9. Not a pawnbroker, but one licensed to appraise and sell household goods. When a landlord took possession of the furniture of those unable to pay rent, the broker would be called in to 'value their goods'. Anti-Semitic caricatures of such brokers, with bowler hats and Disraeli sidelocks, were common in the cartoons of Victorian England, and in novels and plays. 'People hate and scout 'em,' wrote Dickens, 'because they're the ministers of wretchedness, like, to poor people.'

10. A 'billiard-marker' is the employee of a billiard parlour who keeps a record of the game by marking the points made by each player.

I like to think that the crew's Billiard-marker is none other than the billiard-marker whom Sherlock Holmes and his brother Mycroft observed, many years later, strolling down Pall Mall with his friend the Boots. After leaving the Bellman's crew, the Boots had become a private in the Royal Artillery. He was discharged after honourable service in India, but was so fond of his boots that he continued to wear them (as Mycroft noticed) after his retirement from service. (See the story of 'The Greek Interpreter' in *Memoirs of Sherlock Holmes*. For the friendship between Holmes and Carroll, see William S. Baring-Gould, *Sherlock Holmes of Baker Street*, Clarkson Potter, 1962, pages 26–7.)

There was also a Beaver, that paced on the deck,
　　Or would sit making lace in the bow:
And had often (the Bellman said) saved them from wreck,
　　Though none of the sailors knew how.

There was one who was famed for the number of things
　　He forgot when he entered the ship:
His umbrella, his watch, all his jewels and rings,
　　And the clothes he had bought for the trip.

He had forty-two boxes, all carefully packed,
　　With his name painted clearly on each:[11]
But, since he omitted to mention the fact,
　　They were all left behind on the beach.

The loss of his clothes hardly mattered, because
　　He had seven coats on when he came,
With three pair of boots – but the worst of it was,
　　He had wholly forgotten his name.[12]

11. Five of these forty-two boxes can be observed through the window in the illustration on page 65; unfortunately the picture is not clear enough to make out the name painted on two of the boxes. For the meaning of these boxes and the probable name of their owner, see Fit 3, Note 29. Observe, on the opposite page, that the Baker is sitting on what appears to be one of his boxes. If so, all were *not* left behind on the beach.

12. The illustration for this scene deserves careful study. Above deck, left to right, are the Bellman (with a wart on his nose), the Baker (wearing his seven coats and three pairs of boots) and the Barrister. Below deck, left to right: the Billiard-marker, the Banker, the Bonnet-maker (he is making a lady's bonnet), and the Broker.

The Banker's balance scale is for weighing gold, and the loose silver mentioned in Fit 4 (page 70, line 6).

He had wholly forgotten his name

He would answer to 'Hi!' or to any loud cry,
  Such as 'Fry me!' or 'Fritter my wig!'[13]
To 'What-you-may-call-um!' or 'What-was-his-name!'
  But especially 'Thing-um-a-jig!'

While, for those who preferred a more forcible word,
  He had different names from these:
His intimate friends called him 'Candle-ends',
  And his enemies 'Toasted-cheese.'[14]

Such scales were used in Victorian banks for just this purpose. The Broker is holding his walking cane so that the handle touches his lips. I am indebted to Leigh Mercer, of London, for informing me of the fact that this practice, known as cane sucking, was a common affectation of Victorian fops. London dandies, with canes at their lips, are depicted in many cartoons of the time (e.g., see *Punch*, Volume 66, 1874, page 141). See also William Maw Egley's 1859 painting, 'Omnibus Life in London', reproduced in *The Victorian Scene*, by Nicolas Bentley, New York Graphic Society, 1968.

Holiday, in a 1922 letter to a New York purchaser of some of his original *Snark* sketches, disclosed that his first sketch of the Broker 'was intended to give a caricature of a vulgar specimen of the profession, but Lewis Carroll took exception to this and asked me to treat the head in a less aggressive manner. ... I consider that [the first sketch] has much more character, but I understood L. Carroll's objection, and agreed to tone him down.' (The letter is in the Morris Parrish collection, Princeton University Library.)

Holiday's initials, H.H., appear at bottom centre of the picture.

13. 'Fry me' and 'fritter my wig' are expressions that probably were invented by Carroll; at least I have found no evidence that they were common slang expressions of the time. However, *The Oxford English Dictionary* quotes an old Cornish proverb, 'Fry me for a fool and you'll lose your fat in the frying' (citing a reference in *Notes and Queries*, a publication that Carroll read), so it is possible that Carroll had this proverb in mind.

'Fritter my wig' evidently means to mix a wig with batter and fry it in oil or lard to make wig fritters.

'His form is ungainly – his intellect small –'
(So the Bellman would often remark)
'But his courage is perfect! And that, after all,
Is the thing that one needs with a Snark.'

He would joke with hyænas,[15] returning their stare
With an impudent wag of the head:
And he once went a walk, paw-in-paw, with a bear,
'Just to keep up its spirits,' he said.

An alternate meaning: to tear a wig into small pieces. In Carroll's time, sailors referred to shredded sails as frittered.

14. J. A. Lindon, a British word-puzzle expert, calls my attention to the curious fact that 'Candle-ends' (stumps of burned-down candles), 'Toasted-cheese', 'Fry me', and 'Fritter my wig' all refer to objects that are heated. A baker, of course, uses heat in baking, but I incline to the view that the nicknames reflect the crew's awareness that the Baker was perpetually overheated. Although the ship travelled in 'tropical climes' (see Fit 2: page 57, line 11, and note that a hot climate is also suggested by Hope's scanty attire in the picture on page 69), the Baker insisted on wearing seven coats and three pairs of boots. This would surely keep him as warm as toasted cheese. Evidently he dreaded the loss of his body heat as much as he dreaded the loss of his existence. The name Candle-ends may imply that the Baker is about to burn himself out.

15. The species of hyena referred to here is clearly the striped hyena, or laughing hyena, so called because its howl resembles demonic laughter. The Baker later wagged his head at a much more dangerous beast (see Fit 8: page 93, line 11).

He came as a Baker: but owned when too late –
   And it drove the poor Bellman half-mad –
He could only bake Bridecake[16] – for which, I may state,
   No materials were to be had.

The last of the crew needs especial remark,
   Though he looked an incredible dunce:
He had just one idea – but, that one being 'Snark',
   The good Bellman engaged him at once.

He came as a Butcher: [17] but gravely declared,
   When the ship had been sailing a week,
He could only kill Beavers. The Bellman looked scared,
   And was almost too frightened to speak:

But at length he explained, in a tremulous tone,
   There was only one Beaver on board;
And that was a tame one he had of his own,
   Whose death would be deeply deplored.

The Beaver, who happened to hear the remark,
   Protested, with tears in its eyes,
That not even the rapture of hunting the Snark
   Could atone for that dismal surprise!

---

16. Wedding cake.
17. This completes Carroll's description of the ten crew members: Bellman, Boots, Bonnet-maker, Barrister, Broker, Billiard-marker, Banker, Beaver, Baker and Butcher.

To the obvious question of why these names all start with B, including also Boojum and Bandersnatch, there are several possible answers. One is suggested on pages 28–31 of the Introduction. Perhaps

It strongly advised that the Butcher should be
 Conveyed in a separate ship:
But the Bellman declared that would never agree
 With the plans he had made for the trip:

Navigation was always a difficult art,
 Though with only one ship and one bell:
And he feared he must really decline, for his part,
 Undertaking another as well.

The Beaver's best course was, no doubt, to procure
 A second-hand dagger-proof coat —
So the Baker advised it — and next, to insure
 Its life in some Office of note: [18]

This the Banker suggested, and offered for hire
 (On moderate terms), or for sale,
Two excellent Policies, one Against Fire,
 And one Against Damage From Hail.

a better one is suggested by the March Hare at the Mad Tea Party. When Alice asked why the three little (Liddell) sisters drew pictures only of objects that begin with M, the March Hare replied, 'Why not?'

A 1922 letter of Holiday's (the same letter that is quoted from in Note 12), closes with the following postscript: 'I asked Lewis Carroll when I first read his M.S. why he made all the members of the crew have occupations beginning with B. He replied, "Why not?" '

Carroll used the pseudonym 'B.B.' in signing some of his early poems. No one knows why.
18. In England a life insurance company is commonly called an office. 'Office of note' is a company of good repute. 'Hire' in the next line means 'rent'.

Yet still, ever after that sorrowful day,
  Whenever the Butcher was by,
The Beaver kept looking the opposite way,[19]
  And appeared unaccountably shy.

The Beaver kept looking the opposite way

19. In Holiday's illustration for this scene on the ship's bow, note the Butcher's beaver cap. That is not a dagger hanging from his waist; it is a steel for sharpening knives. The Beaver is making lace by the pillow method. A pattern drawn on paper or parchment is placed on the pillow, pins are inserted, and the threads woven by means of small bobbins.

Fit the Second

THE BELLMAN'S SPEECH

THE Bellman himself they all praised to the skies –
  Such a carriage, such ease and such grace!
Such solemnity too! One could see he was wise,
  The moment one looked in his face!

He had bought a large map representing the sea,
  Without the least vestige of land:
And the crew were much pleased when they found it to be
  A map they could all understand.

'What's the good of Mercator's[20] North Poles and Equators,
  Tropics, Zones, and Meridian Lines?'
So the Bellman would cry: and the crew would reply,
  'They are merely conventional signs!

20. Gerhardus Mercator, sixteenth-century Flemish mathematician and cartographer. He devised the method, known as 'Mercator's projection', of projecting a spherical map of the earth on a flat rectangle so that the parallels and meridians become straight lines, and the poles become the rectangle's top and bottom edges.

'Other maps are such shapes, with their islands and capes!
  But we've got our brave Captain to thank'
(So the crew would protest) 'that he's bought *us* the best –
  A perfect and absolute blank!'[21]

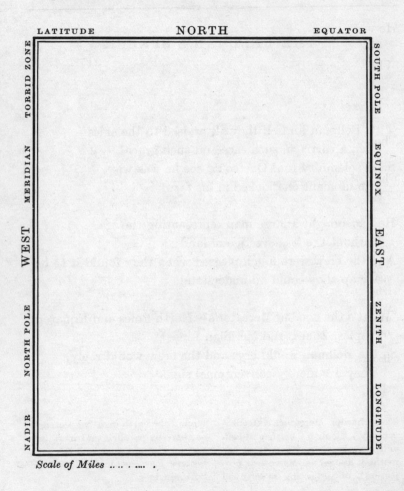

Ocean chart

This was charming, no doubt: but they shortly found out
    That the Captain they trusted so well
Had only one notion for crossing the ocean,
    And that was to tingle his bell.[22]

He was thoughtful and grave – but the orders he gave
    Were enough to bewilder a crew.
When he cried, 'Steer to starboard, but keep her head lar-
      board!'
    What on earth was the helmsman to do?

Then the bowsprit got mixed with the rudder sometimes:[23]
    A thing, as the Bellman remarked,
That frequently happens in tropical climes,
    When a vessel is, so to speak, 'snarked'.

21. In contrast, a map in Carroll's *Sylvie and Bruno Concluded*, Chapter 11, has *everything* on it. The German Professor explains how his country's cartographers experimented with larger and larger maps until they finally made one with a scale of a mile to the mile. 'It has never been spread out, yet,' he says. 'The farmers objected: they said it would cover the whole country, and shut out the sunlight! So now we use the country itself, as its own map, and I assure you it does nearly as well.'
22. This use of the word 'tingle' was common enough in the eighteenth century but already rare in Carroll's day. Perhaps, as correspondent James T. de Kay has observed, Carroll chose this word to evoke subtly the spine-tingling terror that will soon overtake the crew.
23. The bowsprit is a large spar or boom that projects forward from the ship's bow. It can be seen clearly in the illustration on page 44, and behind the Beaver in the picture on page 54. In his preface Carroll explains exactly why the bowsprit occasionally got mixed with the rudder. This confusion is often cited by Freudian critics of Carroll, though they are a bit vague as to just what to make of it.

But the principal failing occurred in the sailing,
  And the Bellman, perplexed and distressed,
Said he *had* hoped, at least, when the wind blew due East
  That the ship would *not* travel due West!

But the danger was past – they had landed at last,
  With their boxes, portmanteaus, and bags:
Yet at first sight the crew were not pleased with the view,
  Which consisted of chasms and crags.

The Bellman perceived that their spirits were low,
  And repeated in musical tone
Some jokes he had kept for a season of woe –
  But the crew would do nothing but groan.

He served out some grog with a liberal hand,
  And bade them sit down on the beach:
And they could not but own that their Captain looked grand,
  As he stood and delivered his speech.

'Friends, Romans, and countrymen, lend me your ears!'[24]
  (They were all of them fond of quotations:
So they drank to his health, and they gave him three cheers,
  While he served out additional rations.)

---

24. Surely no reader will fail to recognize this opening line of Mark Antony's oration at Caesar's funeral, in Shakespeare's *Julius Caesar*.

'We have sailed many months, we have sailed many weeks
    (Four weeks to the month you may mark),
But never as yet ('tis your Captain who speaks)
    Have we caught the least glimpse of a Snark!

'We have sailed many weeks, we have sailed many days
    (Seven days to the week I allow),
But a Snark, on the which we might lovingly gaze,
    We have never beheld till now!

'Come, listen, my men, while I tell you again
    The five unmistakable marks
By which you may know, wheresoever you go,
    The warranted genuine Snarks.

'Let us take them in order. The first is the taste,
    Which is meagre and hollow, but crisp:
Like a coat that is rather too tight in the waist,
    With a flavour of Will-o'-the-wisp.

'Its habit of getting up late you'll agree
    That it carries too far, when I say
That it frequently breakfasts at five-o'clock tea,
    And dines on the following day.

'The third is its slowness in taking a jest.
    Should you happen to venture on one,
It will sigh like a thing that is deeply distressed:
    And it always looks grave at a pun.

'The fourth is its fondness for bathing-machines,[25]
 Which it constantly carries about,
And believes that they add to the beauty of scenes –
 A sentiment open to doubt.

'The fifth is ambition. It next will be right
 To describe each particular batch:
Distinguishing those that have feathers, and bite,
 From those that have whiskers, and scratch.

'For, although common Snarks do no manner of harm,
 Yet I feel it my duty to say,
Some are Boojums–'[26] The Bellman broke off in alarm,
 For the Baker had fainted away.

---

25. Bathing-machines were individual wooden locker rooms on wheels. While the modest Victorian bather changed to bathing clothes, horses would pull the machine into several feet of water. He or she would then emerge through a door facing the sea, screened by a large awning attached to the machine. At many beaches a guide or 'dipper' would forcibly assist the reluctant bather to make the icy plunge.

In one of Carroll's playful letters to Gertrude Chataway he proposes visiting her at Sandown, the summer resort where they first met. If she is unable to find a room for him, he expects her to give him *her* room and to spend the night by herself on the beach. 'If you . . . feel a little chilly, of course you could go into a bathing-machine, which everybody knows is *very* comfortable to sleep in – you know they make the floor of soft wood on purpose. I send you seven kisses (to last a week). . . .'

There are many references to bathing-machines in Victorian literature. The Lord Chancellor, in the Gilbert and Sullivan operetta *Iolanthe*, sings about 'lying awake with a dreadful headache' and dreaming of crossing the channel in rough weather on a steamer from Harwich that is 'something between a large bathing-machine and a very small second-class carriage'.

For more on bathing-machines, see Chapter 2, Note 6, of *Alice's Adventures in Wonderland*, in *The*

Annotated Alice; and *The English Seaside* by H. G. Stokes, 1947, pages 17–25.

26. In Chapter 24 of *Sylvie and Bruno Concluded*, the second half of Carroll's long, sentimental fantasy novel (the first half was published thirteen years after the *Snark*), the following dialogue occurs:

The Professor sighed, and gave it up. 'Do you know what a Boojum is?'

'*I* know!' cried Bruno. 'It's the thing that wrenches people out of their boots!'

'He means "bootjack",' Sylvie explained in a whisper.

'You can't wrench people out of *boots*,' the Professor mildly observed.

Bruno laughed saucily. 'Oo *can*, though! Unless they're *welly* tight in.'

'Once upon a time there was a Boojum –' the Professor began, but stopped suddenly. 'I forget the rest of the Fable,' he said. 'And there was a lesson to be learned from it. I'm afraid I forget *that*, too.'

Various attempts have been made to explain the word *Boojum*. Eric Partridge in his essay on 'The Nonsense Words in Edward Lear and Lewis Carroll' (*Here, There and Everywhere*, London, 1950) suggests that it packs together *Boo!* and *fee, fo, fi, fum!* Phyllis Greenacre points out that in addition to suggesting *Boo!* it also suggests *boohoo*. One thinks also of *boogieman*, though in Carroll's England it was pronounced with a long 'o' and spelled *bogy* or *bogey*. The Old Bogy was the Devil, and a bogy was an evil goblin or anything that aroused terror. The Bogyman was supposed to 'get' little children if they misbehaved.

Boojum is now a common vernacular name for a slithy, queer-shaped tree that thrives only in the central desert of Mexico's Baja California. Joseph Wood Krutch, in his book *The Forgotten Peninsula* (1961), devotes an entire chapter to the boojum. What does it look like? Answers Krutch: like nothing else on earth. Natives call it a *cirio* (wax candle) because it resembles a candle, though its body is covered with what from a distance seems to be a rough hairy growth but on closer inspection proves to be a stubble of short twigs. 'Perhaps only a botanist could love it,' writes Krutch. Fully grown specimens reach a height of fifty feet, sometimes drooping over in an arch until the tip touches the ground. Standing in a forest of boojums, Krutch found the effect hallucinatory, like a surrealist dream.

The name *boojum* was given to the tree by the British ecologist Godfrey Sykes when he explored the Baja in 1922. Like Carroll's Banker, Sykes carried with him a telescope. According to his son's account, he focused his telescope on a distant tree, gazed intently for a few moments, then said, 'Ho, ho, a boojum, definitely a boojum.'

Fit the Third

THE BAKER'S TALE

THEY roused him with muffins – they roused him with ice –
   They roused him with mustard and cress –[27]
They roused him with jam and judicious advice –
   They set him conundrums to guess.

When at length he sat up and was able to speak,
   His sad story he offered to tell;
And the Bellman cried 'Silence! not even a shriek!'
   And excitedly tingled his bell.

There was silence supreme! Not a shriek, not a scream,
   Scarcely even a howl or a groan,
As the man they called 'Ho!' told his story of woe
   In an antediluvian tone.[28]

27. Mustard-and-cress, a common salad and sandwich ingredient in England, is grown from a mixture of the seeds of white mustard and garden cress. When the shoots are about an inch tall, they are cut with scissors and placed between thin slices of bread to make sandwiches for four o'clock tea.

28. Eric Partridge calls attention to this line as one of those rare instances in which Carroll uses a standard word in a completely whimsical sense. Such words occur

'My father and mother were honest, though poor – '
  'Skip all that!' cried the Bellman in haste.
'If it once becomes dark, there's no chance of a Snark –
  We have hardly a minute to waste!'

'I skip forty years,' [29] said the Baker, in tears,
  'And proceed without further remark
To the day when you took me aboard of your ship
  To help you in hunting the Snark.

often in Lear's verse (e.g., 'That intrinsic old man of Peru', 'He weareth a runcible hat', 'Sweetly susceptible blue', 'Propitious old man with a beard').

29. The skipping of 40 years puts the Baker in his early forties. Carroll began writing the *Snark* in 1874 when he was 42. Could the Baker be Carroll himself? J. A. Lindon suggests that the Baker's 42 boxes (Fit 1: page 48, line 9) are perhaps intended to represent Carroll's 42 years. Each box bore the Baker's name and all were left behind when he joined the Snark-hunting expedition. Note also the mention of Rule 42 in Carroll's preface, and the King's remarks at the trial of the Knave of Hearts (*Alice's Adventures in Wonderland*, Chapter 12), 'Rule Forty-two. All persons more than a mile high to leave the court.' Curiously, Carroll refers to his age as 42 in his poem *Phantasmagoria* (Canto 1, Stanza 16) though at the time this poem was written he was still in his thirties. The number 42 certainly seems to have had some sort of special significance for Carroll.

Other passages suggest that Carroll was satirizing himself in the person of the Baker. The Baker's ungainly form and small intellect, his absent-mindedness, his pseudonyms, his tidy packing of boxes, his ways of joking with hyenas and walking with bears, his waggishness, his wakeful nights, his vanishing in the midst of laughter and glee – all add up to a whimsical, funny-sad, self-deprecating portrait.

'A dear uncle of mine (after whom I was named)
  Remarked, when I bade him farewell –'
'Oh, skip your dear uncle!' the Bellman exclaimed,
  As he angrily tingled his bell.

'He remarked to me then,' said that mildest of men,
  ' "If your Snark be a Snark, that is right:
Fetch it home by all means – you may serve it with greens,
  And it's handy for striking a light.[30]

' "You may seek it with thimbles – and seek it with care;
  You may hunt it with forks and hope;
You may threaten its life with a railway-share;
  You may charm it with smiles and soap –" '

('That's exactly the method,' the Bellman bold
  In a hasty parenthesis cried,
'That's exactly the way I have always been told
  That the capture of Snarks should be tried!')

' "But oh, beamish[31] nephew, beware of the day,
  If your Snark be a Boojum! For then
You will softly and suddenly vanish away,
  And never be met with again!"

30. Carroll may have intended this to suggest that the Snark breathes out fire like a dragon, or possibly that the beast's hide is a rough surface on which matches can be struck.
31. This is the first use in the *Snark* of a nonsense word from 'Jabberwocky' (Chapter 1 of *Through the Looking-Glass*). The word is not exactly nonsense: *The Oxford English Dictionary* traces it back to 1530 as a variant of *beaming*.

'But oh, beamish nephew, beware of the day'

'It is this, it is this that oppresses my soul,
    When I think of my uncle's last words:[32]
And my heart is like nothing so much as a bowl
    Brimming over with quivering curds!

'It is this, it is this –' 'We have had that before!'
    The Bellman indignantly said.
And the Baker replied, 'Let me say it once more.
    It is this, it is this that I dread!

'I engage with the Snark – every night after dark –
    In a dreamy delirious fight:
I serve it with greens in those shadowy scenes,
    And I use it for striking a light;

'But if ever I meet with a Boojum, that day,
    In a moment (of this I am sure),
I shall softly and suddenly vanish away –
    And the notion I cannot endure!'

32. Apparently Holiday interpreted 'last words' to mean that the Baker's uncle died after speaking them. At any rate, he pictures the uncle as confined to bed, hands crippled by arthritis, his medicine on a shelf above.

Fit the Fourth

THE HUNTING

The Bellman looked uffish,[33] and wrinkled his brow.
  'If only you'd spoken before!
It's excessively awkward to mention it now,
  With the Snark, so to speak, at the door!

'We should all of us grieve, as you well may believe,
  If you never were met with again –
But surely, my man, when the voyage began,
  You might have suggested it then?

'It's excessively awkward to mention it now –
  As I think I've already remarked.'
And the man they called 'Hi!' replied, with a sigh,
  'I informed you the day we embarked.

33. *Uffish* appears in 'Jabber-wocky'. In a letter to a child friend, Maud Standen, Carroll says that the word suggests to him 'a state of mind when the voice is gruffish, the manner roughish, and the temper huffish'.

'You may charge me with murder – or want of sense –
  (We are all of us weak at times):
But the slightest approach to a false pretence
  Was never among my crimes!

'I said it in Hebrew – I said it in Dutch –
  I said it in German and Greek:
But I wholly forgot (and it vexes me much)
  That English is what you speak!'

' 'Tis a pitiful tale,' said the Bellman, whose face
  Had grown longer at every word:
'But, now that you've stated the whole of your case,
  More debate would be simply absurd.

'The rest of my speech' (he explained to his men)
  'You shall hear when I've leisure to speak it.
But the Snark is at hand, let me tell you again!
  'Tis your glorious duty to seek it!

'To seek it with thimbles, to seek it with care;
  To pursue it with forks and hope;
To threaten its life with a railway-share;
  To charm it with smiles and soap!

'For the Snark's a peculiar creature, that won't
  Be caught in a commonplace way.
Do all that you know, and try all that you don't:
  Not a chance must be wasted to-day!

'*To pursue it with forks and hope*'

'For England expects – I forbear to proceed:
　'Tis a maxim tremendous, but trite:[34]
And you'd best be unpacking the things that you need
　To rig yourselves out for the fight.'

Then the Banker endorsed a blank cheque (which he crossed),
　And changed his loose silver for notes.
The Baker with care combed his whiskers and hair,[35]
　And shook the dust out of his coats.

The Boots and the Broker were sharpening a spade –
　Each working the grindstone in turn;
But the Beaver went on making lace, and displayed
　No interest in the concern:

Though the Barrister tried to appeal to its pride,
　And vainly proceeded to cite
A number of cases, in which making laces
　Had been proved an infringement of right.

34. The tremendous but trite maxim is, of course, 'England expects every man to do his duty.' It was a flag signal to the fleet, ordered by Horatio Nelson shortly before he was killed by a musket shot at the battle of Trafalgar in 1805. According to one account of the episode, Nelson first ordered the signal 'Nelson confides that every man will do his duty.' An officer suggested replacing *Nelson* by *England*, and it was pointed out that *expects* was

in the flag code whereas *confides* would have to be spelled out with a flag for each letter. (For details, see *Notes and Queries*, Series 6, Volume 9, pages 261 and 283.)

'If ... England expects every man to do his duty,' Dickens wrote in *Martin Chuzzlewit*, Chapter 43, 'England is the most sanguine country on the face of the earth, and will find itself continually disappointed.'

35. The Baker appears whiskerless

The maker of Bonnets ferociously planned
    A novel arrangement of bows:
While the Billiard-marker with quivering hand
    Was chalking the tip of his nose.

But the Butcher turned nervous, and dressed himself fine,
    With yellow kid gloves and a ruff –
Said he felt it exactly like going to dine,
    Which the Bellman declared was all 'stuff'.[36]

'Introduce me, now there's a good fellow,' he said,
    'If we happen to meet it together!'
And the Bellman, sagaciously nodding his head,
    Said, 'That must depend on the weather.'

The Beaver went simply galumphing[37] about,
    At seeing the Butcher so shy:
And even the Baker, though stupid and stout,
    Made an effort to wink with one eye.

in Holiday's illustrations. Either Holiday failed to note that the Baker combed his whiskers, or Carroll added this stanza after it was too late to alter the art, or there is a small, almost invisible tuft of side whiskers below the Baker's left ear in the illustration on page 69.

36. *Stuff*, a slang equivalent of *rubbish* or *stuff and nonsense*, was current in Carroll's day.

37. *Galumphing*, from 'Jabberwocky', is one of Carroll's portmanteau words that have entered the dictionary. It is a blend of *gallop* and *triumphant*, meaning (according to *The Oxford English Dictionary*) 'to march on exultantly with irregular bounding movements'. 'Both Carroll and Lear,' writes Eric Partridge, 'must, in their philological heaven, be chortling at the thought that they have frabjously galumphed their way into the English vocabulary.'

'Be a man!' said the Bellman in wrath, as he heard
  The Butcher beginning to sob.
'Should we meet with a Jubjub,[38] that desperate bird,
  We shall need all our strength for the job!'

38. 'Beware the Jubjub bird,' so reads a line in the second stanza of 'Jabberwocky'. Eric Partridge thinks *Jubjub* may be a pun on *jug*, an English word expressing one of the notes of the nightingale; perhaps a blend of *jug-jug* and *hubbub*.

Fit the Fifth

THE BEAVER'S LESSON

THEY sought it with thimbles, they sought it with care;
  They pursued it with forks and hope;[39]
They threatened its life with a railway-share;
  They charmed it with smiles and soap.[40]

39. Elspeth Huxley gave the title *With Forks and Hope* to her African notebook, published in the United States by Morrow in 1964.

40. This is the third appearance of this stanza but the first to describe the actual carrying out of the Snark-hunting method advised by the Baker's uncle. (For translations of the stanza into French, Latin, and Italian, see the annotated bibliography.) The fact that essentially the same stanza occurs altogether six times in the poem has led some to suspect that it may conceal a private, cryptic message. If so, the message has never been decoded.

My theory – the reader may be able to formulate a better one – is that thimbles, forks, a railway share, smiles, and soap are connected with the Snark's five unmistakable marks mentioned in Fit 2. The forks are for eating crisp Snark meat. The railway share appeals to the Snark's ambition to become wealthy and so can be used for baiting a death trap. Smiles are to let the Snark know when a pun has been perpetrated. The soap is of course for the bathing machines that the Snark carries about, and the thimble is used for thumping the side of the creature's head to wake him in time for five-o'clock tea.

The bare-bosomed young woman in Holiday's illustration for this stanza is Hope. (She may also be the ship's wooden figurehead. See the illustration on page 44.) It is amusing to note that when Andrew Lang reviewed the *Snark* in 1876 he failed completely to identify the young lady. 'In a sketch of the whole crew,' he wrote, 'there is a really graceful half-draped female figure with an anchor and a trident, who may or may not be the Bonnet-maker, but who would deeply shock the Banker at her side.'

It is not by accident that Holiday placed a sheet anchor on Hope's shoulder. As far back as the sixteenth century, the term 'sheet anchor' has been figuratively used for that on which one ultimately relies: one's mainstay, after all else has failed. Artists in England traditionally depicted Hope with such an anchor.

The woman with bowed head is Care. (She is also mentioned in the opening stanza of the poem; the Bellman lands her with the crew.) There are five 'forks' in the picture if we count Hope's anchor as a fork. In the upper left corner are the Broker, still sucking his cane, and the Baker. The Barrister is wearing his wig and legal robes. The Banker carries a tuning fork (appropriate, as J. A. Lindon suggests, to a man who deals in notes) and the telescope that he is seen holding in the book's first illustration. The Beaver holds a microscope.

Carroll does not mention either the microscope or telescope. Perhaps the Beaver is searching for microscopic clues, such as a bit of feather or whisker, and the Banker hopes to spot a Snark in the far distance. The instruments are also appropriate, as Lindon has observed, to the habits of the two crew members: a Banker must constantly be looking ahead on his investments, whereas a Beaver is concerned only with what is directly under its nose. (Cf. the railway scene in *Through the Looking-Glass*, in which the Guard looks at Alice first through a telescope, then through a microscope.)

When Holiday sent Carroll a sketch of this scene, Carroll replied that he admired Hope and Care, but thought they dulled his point: the mixing of two meanings of the word *with*. Holiday replied: 'Precisely, and I intended to add a third —"in company with" – and so develop the point.' Carroll assented.

In a later letter to Holiday, Carroll wrote: 'I agree with you in thinking the head of Hope a great success; it is quite lovely.' He proposed that Holiday do a special cover, for a more expensive edition of the book, with Hope on the front, Care on the back. 'What do you think of surrounding them,' he asked, 'one with a border of interlaced forks, the other with a shower of thimbles?' Apparently these cover pictures were never made; at any rate, the book was published in only one edition, with the two cover pictures reproduced on pages 122 and 126 of this volume.

(The letters mentioned in the two paragraphs above are quoted by Henry Holiday in his article on 'The Snark's Significance'. See bibliography.)

Then the Butcher contrived an ingenious plan
    For making a separate sally;
And had fixed on a spot unfrequented by man,
    A dismal and desolate valley.

But the very same plan to the Beaver occurred:
    It had chosen the very same place;
Yet neither betrayed, by a sign or a word,
    The disgust that appeared in his face.

Each thought he was thinking of nothing but 'Snark'
    And the glorious work of the day;
And each tried to pretend that he did not remark[41]
    That the other was going that way.

But the valley grew narrow and narrower still,
    And the evening got darker and colder,
Till (merely from nervousness, not from goodwill)
    They marched along shoulder to shoulder.

Then a scream, shrill and high, rent the shuddering sky,
    And they knew that some danger was near:
The Beaver turned pale to the tip of its tail,
    And even the Butcher felt queer.

41. 'Remark' in the sense of *observe*
or *notice*, not in the sense of making
a remark.

He thought of his childhood, left far far behind –
    That blissful and innocent state –
The sound so exactly recalled to his mind
    A pencil that squeaks on a slate!

' 'Tis the voice of the Jubjub!'[42] he suddenly cried.
    (This man, that they used to call 'Dunce'.)
'As the Bellman would tell you,' he added with pride,
    'I have uttered that sentiment once.

' 'Tis the note of the Jubjub! Keep count, I entreat;
    You will find I have told it you twice.
'Tis the song of the Jubjub! The proof is complete,
    If only I've stated it thrice.'

The Beaver had counted with scrupulous care,
    Attending to every word:
But it fairly lost heart, and outgrabe[43] in despair,
    When the third repetition occurred.

It felt that, in spite of all possible pains,
    It had somehow contrived to lose count,
And the only thing now was to rack its poor brains
    By reckoning up the amount.

42. Cf. ' 'Tis the voice of the Lobster' (*Alice's Adventures in Wonderland*, Chapter 10), Carroll's parody on Isaac Watts's poem ' 'Tis the voice of the sluggard.' All three lines derive ultimately from the Biblical phrase (Song of Solomon 2:12) 'the voice of the turtle'.

43. *Outgrabe* is from the first stanza of 'Jabberwocky'. Humpty Dumpty explains that *outgribing* 'is something between bellowing and whist-

'Two added to one – if that could but be done,'
  It said, 'with one's fingers and thumbs!'
Recollecting with tears how, in earlier years,
  It had taken no pains with its sums.

'The thing can be done,' said the Butcher, 'I think.
  The thing must be done, I am sure.
The thing shall be done! Bring me paper and ink,
  The best there is time to procure.'

The Beaver brought paper, portfolio, pens,[44]
  And ink in unfailing supplies:
While strange creepy creatures came out of their dens,
  And watched them with wondering eyes.

ling, with a kind of sneeze in the middle: however, you'll hear it done, maybe – down in the wood yonder – and, when you've once heard it, you'll be *quite* content.'
44. J. A. Lindon suggests the illustration for this scene (page 79) may have been intended as one of those puzzle pictures in which you try to spot as many objects as you can that begin with a certain letter. Here, of course, the letter is B. The list includes: Butcher, Beaver, Bellman, bell, barrel organs, bats, bugles, band, bottles, books, brace and bit. Perhaps the reader can find others.

The picture has many fascinating details. Note the lizard labelled 'income tax' that is rifling the Butcher's pockets. The kittens are playing with the Butcher's yellow kid gloves. The large object in the lower right corner is an ornate inkstand called a 'standish'.

Colenso's *Arithmetic*, at the Butcher's feet, was a popular schoolbook of the day. It was written by Bishop (note the B!) John William Colenso, one of the great controversial figures of the Victorian era. He began his career as a mathematical tutor and author of a series of mathematics textbooks widely used throughout England. In 1846 he was appointed Bishop of Natal, a South African province where the native Zulus badgered him with embarrassing questions about the Old Testament. The more Colenso pondered his answers the more he

So engrossed was the Butcher, he heeded them not,
   As he wrote with a pen in each hand,
And explained all the while in a popular style
   Which the Beaver could well understand.

'Taking Three as the subject to reason about –
   A convenient number to state –
We add Seven, and Ten, and then multiply out
   By One Thousand diminished by Eight.

convinced himself that Christianity was lost if it continued to insist on the Bible's historical accuracy. He expressed these heretical views in a series of books, using arithmetical arguments to prove the nonsense of various Old Testament tales. How, for example, could 12,000 Israelites slaughter 200,000 Midianites? This atrocity, the bishop decided, 'had happily only been carried out on paper'. Such opinions seem mild today, but at the time they touched off a tempest that rocked the English church. Colenso was savagely denounced, socially ostracized, and finally excommunicated, though the courts decided in his favour and he was later reinstated at Natal.

It is appropriate that the second book in Holiday's illustration is *On the Reductio Ad Absurdum*. Just as Carroll reduced the sea ballad to absurdity, so Colenso reduced to absurdity the literal interpretation of the Bible. Was Carroll pro or con Colenso? I have been unable to find out. He surely would have sided with the bishop in his attacks on the doctrine of eternal punishment, but it is doubtful if he would have favoured Colenso's defence of polygamy among Zulu converts or the degree to which the bishop dismissed Biblical stories as mythology.

For a recent article on Colenso see 'The Colenso Controversy', by P. O. G. White in *Theology*, vol. 65, October 1962, pages 402–8.

The winged pigs derive from the old Scottish proverb, 'Pigs may fly, but it's not likely'. 'Just about as much right as pigs have to fly,' says the Duchess in the first *Alice* book (Chapter 9), and in the second book (Chapter 4) Tweedledee sings:

And why the sea is boiling hot –
And whether pigs have wings.

The Beaver brought paper, portfolio, pens

'The result we proceed to divide, as you see,
    By Nine Hundred and Ninety and Two:
Then subtract Seventeen, and the answer must be
    Exactly and perfectly true.[45]

'The method employed I would gladly explain,
    While I have it so clear in my head,
If I had but the time and you had but the brain –
    But much yet remains to be said.

'In one moment I've seen what has hitherto been
    Enveloped in absolute mystery,
And without extra charge I will give you at large
    A Lesson in Natural History.'[46]

---

45. It is good to have clearly in mind what is going on here. The Butcher is fairly certain that he has made his statement three times; according to the Bellman's rule-of-three, this proves the truth of his assertion. The Beaver counted the first two statements, but had difficulty adding them to the last one. The Butcher is proving to the Beaver that 2 plus 1 does in fact equal 3. His arithmetic procedure is a sterling example of circular reasoning. It begins with 3, the number he seeks to prove, and ends with 3; but the procedure is such that he is certain to end with whatever number he starts with. If x be the starting number, the procedure can be expressed algebraically as:

$$\frac{(x + 7 + 10)(1000 - 8)}{992} - 17$$

which simplifies to x.

46. Phyllis Greenacre thinks that the ten members of the crew represent the ten children in the Dodgson family, with Charles as the Baker. 'The part of the poem in which the Butcher gives the docile Beaver a lesson in natural history,' she writes, 'is probably [analysts often have difficulty writing 'possibly'] but a thinly disguised picture of a consultation among the little Dodgsons regarding the mysterious [sex] life of their awesome parents.'

In his genial way he proceeded to say
    (Forgetting all laws of propriety,
And that giving instruction, without introduction,
    Would have caused quite a thrill in Society),

'As to temper the Jubjub's a desperate bird,
    Since it lives in perpetual passion:
Its taste in costume is entirely absurd –
    It is ages ahead of the fashion:

'But it knows any friend it has met once before:
    It never will look at a bribe:
And in charity-meetings it stands at the door,
    And collects – though it does not subscribe.

'Its flavour when cooked is more exquisite far
    Than mutton, or oysters, or eggs:
(Some think it keeps best in an ivory jar,
    And some, in mahogany kegs:)

'You boil it in sawdust: you salt it in glue:
    You condense it with locusts and tape:
Still keeping one principal object in view –
    To preserve its symmetrical shape.' [47]

47. H. S. M. Coxeter, professor of mathematics at the University of Toronto, has called my attention to a geometrical interpretation given to this stanza by the English mathematician John Leech. The stanza tells how to saw and glue together the wooden rods for a model of the skeletal framework of a regular polyhedron. For *locusts* read *locuses* or *loci*, for *tape* read *tape measure*.

The Butcher would gladly have talked till next day,
　　But he felt that the Lesson must end,
And he wept with delight in attempting to say
　　He considered the Beaver his friend.

While the Beaver confessed, with affectionate looks
　　More eloquent even than tears,
It had learnt in ten minutes far more than all books
　　Would have taught it in seventy years.

They returned hand-in-hand, and the Bellman, unmanned
　　(For a moment) with noble emotion,
Said, 'This amply repays all the wearisome days
　　We have spent on the billowy ocean!'

Such friends, as the Beaver and Butcher became,
　　Have seldom if ever been known;
In winter or summer, 'twas always the same –
　　You could never meet either alone.[48]

And when quarrels arose – as one frequently finds
　　Quarrels will, spite of every endeavour –
The song of the Jubjub recurred to their minds,
　　And cemented their friendship for ever!

48. I had always assumed that the Butcher and Beaver became a pair of ship buddies until I read Andrew Lang's review of the *Snark*. 'The drawing of the Beaver sitting at her bobbins is very satisfactory,' Lang writes, 'the natural shyness of the Beaver in the presence of the Butcher being admirably rendered.' The thought that the Beaver might be a 'she' is rather startling. Carroll always refers to the Beaver alone with neutral pronouns.

Fit the Sixth

THE BARRISTER'S DREAM [49]

THEY sought it with thimbles, they sought it with care;
  They pursued it with forks and hope;
They threatened its life with a railway-share;
  They charmed it with smiles and soap.

49. The farcical side of English law had received its classic expression in 1837 in Dickens's story, in *The Pickwick Papers*, of Mr Pickwick's trial for breach of promise; a trial that may have influenced Carroll's equally celebrated account of the trial of the Knave of Hearts, perhaps also the Barrister's dream.

Another possible influence on the dream was the trial of the Tichborne claimant. Sir Roger Charles Tichborne, a wealthy young Englishman, was lost at sea in 1854 when the ship on which he sailed went down with all hands. His eccentric dowager mother, Lady Tichborne, refused to believe that her son had drowned. She foolishly advertised for news of Sir Roger and, sure enough, in 1865 an illiterate butcher in Wagga Wagga, New South Wales,

responded. Sir Roger had been a slim man with straight black hair. The butcher was extremely fat, with wavy brown light hair. Nevertheless, there was a big emotional recognition scene when mother and claimant finally met in Paris. The trustees of Sir Roger's estate were unconvinced. They brought suit against the claimant in 1871 and the trial turned into one of the longest and funniest of all English court cases. More than a hundred persons swore that the claimant was indeed Sir Roger. Lewis Carroll followed the trial with interest, recording in his diary on 28 February 1874, the final verdict of guilty and the claimant's sentence of fourteen years for perjury.

It is possible that Carroll intended the Barrister's Dream to be a satire

But the Barrister, weary of proving in vain
   That the Beaver's lace-making was wrong,[50]
Fell asleep, and in dreams saw the creature quite plain
   That his fancy had dwelt on so long.

He dreamed that he stood in a shadowy Court,
   Where the Snark, with a glass in its eye,
Dressed in gown, bands, and wig,[51] was defending a pig
   On the charge of deserting its sty.

The Witnesses proved, without error or flaw.
   That the sty was deserted when found:
And the Judge kept explaining the state of the law
   In a soft under-current of sound.

The indictment had never been clearly expressed,
   And it seemed that the Snark had begun,
And had spoken three hours, before any one guessed
   What the pig was supposed to have done.

on some of the episodes in the Tichborne case, and there is little doubt that Holiday's Barrister is a caricature of Edward Kenealy, counsel for the claimant (cf. the cartoon of Kenealy in *Punch*, Volume 68, 1875, page 91). All this, together with the presence of a Butcher in Carroll's crew, gave rise to a popular interpretation of the poem: that it was throughout intended as a satire on the Tichborne case. (See *The Tichborne Claimant* by Douglas Woodruff, Farrar Straus and Cudahy, 1957.

50. See Fit 4: page 70, line 11.

51. Note the contrast between the appearance of the Snark in the Barrister's dream – thin, with pointed head, ridged back, three fingers and thumb – and the actual Snark in Holiday's suppressed picture. Of course the Barrister is only dreaming; also, we must remember that there are several species of Snark.

'Bands' refers to the traditional pair of projecting cloth strips which you see attached to the Snark's gown below his wig.

The Jury had each formed a different view
    (Long before the indictment was read),
And they all spoke at once, so that none of them knew
    One word that the others had said.

'*You must know –*' said the Judge: but the Snark exclaimed, '*Fudge!*'

'You must know –' said the Judge: but the Snark exclaimed,
   'Fudge![52]
   That statute is obsolete quite!
Let me tell you, my friends, the whole question depends
   On an ancient manorial right.

'In the matter of Treason the pig would appear
   To have aided, but scarcely abetted:
While the charge of Insolvency fails, it is clear,
   If you grant the plea "never indebted" [53]

'The fact of Desertion I will not dispute:
   But its guilt, as I trust, is removed
(So far as relates to the costs of this suit)
   By the Alibi which has been proved.

'My poor client's fate now depends on your votes.'
   Here the speaker sat down in his place,
And directed the Judge to refer to his notes
   And briefly to sum up the case.

52. 'Mr Burchell,' writes Oliver Goldsmith in Chapter 11 of *The Vicar of Wakefield*, '. . . sate with his face turned to the fire, and at the conclusion of every sentence would cry out *fudge*, an expression which displeased us all, and in some measure damped the rising spirits of the conversation.'

Fudge (meaning 'bosh', 'nonsense') was at one time a common expression of British sailors. According to Isaac Disraeli (in his *Notes on the Navy*): 'There was in our time, one Captain Fudge, a commander of a merchant-man; who, upon his return from a voyage, always brought home a good cargo of lies; insomuch that now, aboard ship, the sailors, when they hear a great lie, cry out "*Fudge!*" '

Thomas Bettler informs me that

But the Judge said he never had summed up before;
  So the Snark undertook it instead,
And summed it so well that it came to far more
  Than the Witnesses ever had said!

When the verdict was called for, the Jury declined,
  As the word was so puzzling to spell;
But they ventured to hope that the Snark wouldn't mind
  Undertaking that duty as well.

So the Snark found the verdict, although, as it owned,
  It was spent with the toils of the day:
When it said the word 'GUILTY!' the Jury all groaned,
  And some of them fainted away.

Then the Snark pronounced sentence,[54] the Judge being quite
  Too nervous to utter a word:
When it rose to its feet, there was silence like night,
  And the fall of a pin might be heard.

in the Gilbert and Sullivan operetta, *Trial by Jury* (another famous spoof on English courts), the Judge sings:

  Though all my law is fudge,
  Yet I'll never, never budge,
  But I'll live and die a judge!

53. *Never indebted*, or *nil debet*, is a legal term meaning 'he owes nothing'. It is the plea of the defendant, in a common-law action of debt, by which he denies completely the allegations of the plaintiff.

  R. M. Redheffer and H. P. Young

have called my attention to the amusing circular reasoning in the next stanza. Strictly speaking, an 'alibi' is an assertion of one's absence from the scene of a crime. The Snark argues that his client is not guilty of desertion because it was somewhere else at the time.

54. Cf. the Mouse's tale in Chapter 3 of *Alice's Adventures in Wonderland*, in which Fury (a dog) tells a mouse that he will take him to court and serve as both judge and jury.

'Transportation[55] for life' was the sentence it gave,
    'And *then* to be fined forty pound.'
The Jury all cheered, though the Judge said he feared
    That the phrase was not legally sound.

But their wild exultation was suddenly checked
    When the jailer informed them, with tears,
Such a sentence would have not the slightest effect,
    As the pig had been dead for some years.

The Judge left the Court, looking deeply disgusted:
    But the Snark, though a little aghast,
As the lawyer to whom the defence was intrusted,
    Went bellowing on to the last.

Thus the Barrister dreamed, while the bellowing seemed
    To grow every moment more clear:
Till he woke to the knell of a furious bell,
    Which the Bellman rang close at his ear.

55. 'Transportation' was the deportation of convicts to a British colony where they were herded into penal gangs and exploited for hard labour. Before the United States won its independence, transported convicts from England provided much of the labour (later taken over by Negro slaves) on the large plantations. Protests from the colonies, chiefly Australia, led to the abandonment of the system, and England began a belated building of adequate prisons. By the time the *Snark* was written, transportation had ceased in England, though it was continued by France and other colonial powers.

Fit the Seventh

THE BANKER'S FATE

THEY sought it with thimbles, they sought it with care;
  They pursued it with forks and hope;
They threatened its life with a railway-share;
  They charmed it with smiles and soap.

And the Banker, inspired with a courage so new
  It was matter for general remark,
Rushed madly ahead and was lost to their view
  In his zeal to discover the Snark.

But while he was seeking with thimbles and care,
  A Bandersnatch 56 swiftly drew nigh
And grabbed at the Banker, who shrieked in despair,
  For he knew it was useless to fly.

---

56. The second stanza of 'Jabberwocky' refers to 'the frumious Bandersnatch', and the White King (Chapter 7 of *Through the Looking-Glass*) also speaks of the beast. Eric Partridge thinks the word may combine a suggestion of the animal's snatching proclivities with either *bandog* (a ferocious watch-dog) or *bandar* (Hindustani for rhesus monkey).

He offered large discount – he offered a cheque
    (Drawn 'to bearer') for seven-pounds-ten:
But the Bandersnatch merely extended its neck
    And grabbed at the Banker again.

Without rest or pause – while those frumious[57] jaws
    Went savagely snapping around –
He skipped and he hopped, and he floundered and flopped,
    Till fainting he fell to the ground.

The Bandersnatch fled as the others appeared:
    Led on by that fear-stricken yell:
And the Bellman remarked, 'It is just as I feared!'
    And solemnly tolled on his bell.

He was black in the face, and they scarcely could trace
    The least likeness to what he had been:
While so great was his fright that his waistcoat turned
    white –[58]
    A wonderful thing to be seen!

To the horror of all who were present that day,
    He uprose in full evening dress,
And with senseless grimaces endeavoured to say
    What his tongue could no longer express.

57. *Frumious*, another 'Jabberwocky' word, is fully explained by Carroll in his preface to the *Snark*.
58. Elizabeth Sewell, in her book *The Field of Nonsense*, points out the similarity of this line with a line in an earlier limerick by Edward Lear:

There was an old man of Port Gregor,
Whose actions were noted for vigour;
    He stood on his head,
    Till his waistcoat turned red,
That eclectic old man of Port Gregor.

. . . so great was his fright that his waistcoat turned white

Down he sank in a chair – ran his hands through his hair –
  And chanted in mimsiest[59] tones
Words whose utter inanity proved his insanity,
  While he rattled a couple of bones.[60]

'Leave him here to his fate – it is getting so late!'
  The Bellman exclaimed in a fright.
'We have lost half the day. Any further delay,
  And we shan't catch a Snark before night!'

59. According to Humpty Dumpty, the word *mimsy* (from the first stanza of 'Jabberwocky') is a portmanteau word combining *miserable* and *flimsy*.

60. In Holiday's illustration for this scene we see the Banker, black of face and white of waistcoat, rattling a pair of bones in each hand. In Negro minstrels, popular in Victorian England as well as in the United States and on the Continent, bone castanets were traditionally rattled by Mr Bones (note the B), who occupied one of the end chairs. (Mr Tambo, who played the tambourine, sat in the other end chair.) Alexander L. Taylor, in his study of Carroll (*The White Knight*, 1952), thinks the Banker's fate 'may be a weird caricature of extravagant church ritual', but both Carroll and Holiday obviously have in mind nothing more than Mr Bones.

At the Banker's feet is a piece of sheet music to be played *con imbecillità*. The Butcher is still wearing the ruff and yellow kid gloves that he put on in Fit 4 (page 71, line 6). The scene has the same gibbering nightmarish quality that pervades the final scenes of the two *Alice* books, just before all the dream characters suddenly vanish away.

Note that the Banker has regrown the shock of hair that can be seen on top of his head in the picture on page 49, but which the picture on page 44 shows that he lost before the crew landed.

Fit the Eighth

THE VANISHING

They sought it with thimbles, they sought it with care;
  They pursued it with forks and hope;
They threatened its life with a railway-share;
  They charmed it with smiles and soap.

They shuddered to think that the chase might fail,
  And the Beaver, excited at last,
Went bounding along on the tip of its tail,
  For the daylight was nearly past.

'There is Thingumbob shouting!' the Bellman said.
  'He is shouting like mad, only hark!
He is waving his hands, he is wagging his head,
  He has certainly found a Snark!'

They gazed in delight, while the Butcher exclaimed,
  'He was always a desperate wag!' 61
They beheld him – their Baker – their hero unnamed –
  On the top of a neighbouring crag,

61. The Butcher was thought to be a dunce (Fit 5: page 76, line 6), but recalling how quickly he recognized the voice of the Jubjub, and how he

93

Erect and sublime, for one moment of time.
  In the next, that wild figure they saw
(As if stung by a spasm) plunge into a chasm,
  While they waited and listened in awe.[62]

'It's a Snark!' was the sound that first came to their ears,
  And seemed almost too good to be true.
Then followed a torrent of laughter and cheers:
  Then the ominous words, 'It's a Boo –'[63]

taught the Beaver more in ten minutes than it could have learned from books in seventy years, it is not surprising to find him making a clever pun. (The Baker's habit of wagging his head when confronted by wild animals has already been mentioned in the first fit – page 51, line 6.) The pun reveals great presence of mind on the Butcher's part. The Boojum was undoubtedly so distressed at being unable to see the point of the joke that it was too embarrassed to confront any of the other crew members before they were all saved by the coming of night.

62. 'Many children have some fabled ogre,' writes Phyllis Greenacre (*Swift and Carroll*, page 240), 'often in animal form, or some "secret", with which they scare each other and themselves. This is the antithesis of the imaginary companion whose presence is comforting, strengthening or relieving. Psychoanalysis reveals that it is generally some representation of the primal scene, in which the sexual images of the parents are fused into a frightening or awe-inspiring single figure. This is probably [that word again!] the significance of the *Snark*, in which the last "fit." is an acting out of the primal scene with the Baker first standing "erect and sublime" and then plunging into the chasm between the crags.'

63. Larry Shaw, in a very funny article called 'The Baker Murder Case' (*Inside and Science Fiction Advertiser*, a fan magazine, September 1956, pages 4–12) argues that the *Snark* is a cleverly disguised tale of the murder of the Baker. On the basis of numerous obscure clues, Shaw proves that the Boots was the Snark, and that the Baker tried to reveal this fact by crying 'It's a Boots!' just before the Boots killed him.

Then, silence

Then, silence.[64] Some fancied they heard in the air
  A weary and wandering sigh
That sounded like '– jum!' but the others declare
  It was only a breeze that went by.

They hunted till darkness came on, but they found
  Not a button, or feather, or mark,
By which they could tell that they stood on the ground
  Where the Baker had met with the Snark.

In the midst of the word he was trying to say,
  In the midst of his laughter and glee,
He had softly and suddenly vanished away –
  For the Snark *was* a Boojum, you see.

THE END

64. Holiday's illustration for this scene, showing the Bellman ringing a knell for the passing of the Baker, is quite a remarkable puzzle picture. Thousands of readers must have glanced at this picture without noticing (though they may have shivered with subliminal perception) the huge, almost transparent head of the Baker, abject terror on his features, as a gigantic beak (or is it a claw?) seizes his wrist and drags him into the ultimate darkness.

BIBLIOGRAPHY

EDITIONS OF THE *Snark*

The Hunting of the Snark. Macmillan, 1876.

The first edition had on its front cover the Holiday drawing reprinted here on page 122; on its back cover the drawing reprinted on page 126. Thus the front of the book depicted a bell*man*, the back a bell *buoy*. In his autobiography Holiday tells of having made a sketch of this buoy while on a boat trip from London to Liverpool. 'When Dodgson wanted a motive for the back cover, something that would bear the words "It was a Boojum," I bethought me of my bell-buoy, which exactly met my want.'

The Hunting of the Snark and Other Poems. Harper and Brothers, 1903. Illustrated by Peter Newell.

The Hunting of the Snark. Wausau, Wisconsin, 1897. Illustrated by Gardner C. Teall.

The Hunting of the Snark. Peter Pauper Press, 1939. Illustrated by Carl Cobbledick.

The Hunting of the Snark. Chatto and Windus, 1941. Illustrated by Mervyn Peake.

The Hunting of the Snark. Peter Pauper Press, 1952. Illustrated by Aldren Watson.

The Hunting of the Snark. Pantheon, 1966. Illustrated by Kelly Oechsli.

The Hunting of the Snark. Utrecht, De Roos, 1966. Text in English. Illustrated by Peter Vos.

TRANSLATIONS OF THE *Snark*

La Chasse au Snark. Hours Press, Chapelle Réauville, Eure, 1929. 29 pages. Translated into French by Louis Aragon. Reprinted in 1949 by Pierre Seghers, Paris, 44 pages.

Aragon wrote this pedestrian translation (it has neither rhyme nor metre) when he was a young Bohemian in Paris, associated with the surrealist movement, and shortly before he completed his transition from Snarxism to Marxism to become the leading literary figure of the French Communist Party.

The first manifesto of the French surrealists, written by André Breton in 1924, spoke of Carroll as a surrealist. In 1931 Aragon contributed an essay on Carroll to the French magazine *Le Surréalisme au service de la révolution*, in which he tried to show that Carroll's nonsense writings, disguised as children's books, actually were politically subversive protests against Victorian bourgeois morality and hypocrisy. The essay is remarkable also for its many factual errors (e.g., the statement that Carroll wore a pointed beard), but there is no evidence that Aragon intended it as a joke. In fact, Breton wrote an article in 1939 to refute Aragon's Marxist interpretation of Carrollian nonsense. (See Philip Thody's essay, 'Lewis Carroll and the Surrealists', in the *Twentieth Century*, Volume 163, pages 427–34, May 1958.)

The following sample stanza from Aragon's translation (as well as the stanzas quoted below from other translations) is the 'sought it with thimbles' stanza that begins each of the last four fits.

> Ils le traquèrent avec des gobelets ils le traquèrent avec soin
> Ils le poursuivirent avec des fourches et de l'espoir
> Ils menacèrent sa vie avec une action de chemin de fer
> Ils le charmèrent avec des sourires et du savon

The Hunting of the Snark. Macmillan, 1934. 57 pages. Translated into Latin by Percival Robert Brinton, Rector of Hambleden, Bucks, England.

I have . . . found a certain affinity in character as well as in experience [Brinton writes in his introduction] between the hero of the Aeneid and the hero of 'The Snark'. Both the Bellman and the pious Aeneas were leaders of an adventurous expedition by sea and land: both pursued their quest with simplicity and single-mindedness. Each had devoted followers; each found himself thwarted by a hostile and mysterious power; each has survived to interest later generations in his story.

Mr Brinton's translation is in Vergilian hexameters:

> Spe simul ac furcis, cura et digitalibus usi
> Quaerebant praedam socii: via ferrea monstro
> Letum intentabat: risus sapoque trahebant.

The Hunting of the Snark. Oxford, printed at the Shakespeare Head Press and sold by Basil Blackwell, 1936. 115 pages. Translated into Latin elegiacs by Hubert Digby Watson. Foreword by Gilbert Murray.

The book includes a note by Watson in which he interprets the poem as a search for world peace. 'May not "thimbles" be an allusion to the "Women's peace crusade" and "smiles and soap" to the lip-service of those whose practice seldom comes up to their preaching?' He sees the Baker as a 'mild-mannered Pacifist who is on very friendly terms with the (Russian) Bear, but suffers a great shock when the Peace which he thinks he has discovered turns out to be an army entitled "The International Police Force of the New Commonwealth".'

The Butcher, in Watson's view, is the 'truculent warmonger', the Beaver the isolationist who 'displays no interest in the concern' but eventually becomes the warmonger's bosom friend. The voice of the Jubjub is the screechings of the yellow press. And so on. He concludes on a hopeful note: the new Bellman of England, Stanley Baldwin, has a name that begins with B.

> Cum cura et digiti quaerunt muliebribus armis,
> Cum furcis etiam spe comitante petunt;
> Instrumenta viae ferratae scripta minantur,
> Sapone et fabricant risibus illecebras.

La caccia allo Snarco. Magi-Spinetti, Rome, 1945. 79 pages. Translated into Italian by Cesare Vico Lodovici. Illustrated by Ketty Castellucci.

> Lo cercarono con diligenza, lo cercarono con ditali,
> lo inseguirono con speranza e con forchette;
> gli insidiarono la vita con un'Azione delle 'Meridionali':
> lo incantarono con sorrisi e saponette.

Snarkjakten. Albert Bouniers Forlag, Stockholm, 1959. A Swedish translation with illustrations by Tove Jansen.

Snarkejagten. Det Schønbergske Forlag, Copenhagen, 1963. 77 pages. Translated into Danish by Christopher Maaløe.

La chasse au Snark. Translated into French rhymed verse by Henri Parisot and included in his translation of the two *Alice* books. Flammarion, Paris, 1969.

Die Jagd nach dem Schnark. Translated into German by Klaus Reichert. Insel Verlag, Frankfurt, West Germany, 1972.

NOTE: A German work with the startling title *Die Fahrt der Snark* (Berlin, 1930) turns out to be a translation of Jack London's book *The Cruise of the Snark*, 1908. This is an account of a voyage that London and his wife made around the world in a small boat which London built himself and named the Snark 'because we could not think of any other name'.

CONTEMPORARY REVIEWS OF THE *Snark*

Andrew Lang. The *Academy*, Volume 9, 8 April 1876, pages 326–7.

A generally unfavourable review of both text and pictures. After quoting the stanza about the Snark's slowness in taking a jest and its habit of looking grave at puns, Lang adds: 'To tell the truth, a painful truth it is, this quality of the snark has communicated itself to the reviewer.'

Unsigned. The *Athenaeum*. Volume 67, 8 April 1876, page 495.

It may be that the author of *Alice's Adventures in Wonderland* is still suffering from the attack of Claimant on the brain, which some time ago numbed or distracted so many intellects. Or it may be that he has merely been inspired by a wild desire to reduce to idiocy as many readers, and more especially, reviewers as possible. At all events, he has published what we may consider the most bewildering of modern poems. . . .

ABOUT THE *Snark*

'The Snark's Significance'. The *Academy*, 29 January 1898, pages 128–30. Short articles by Henry Holiday, M.H.T., and St. J.E.C.H.

Bibliography

'A Commentary on the Snark'. Snarkophilus Snobbs (F. Ċ. S. Schiller). *Mind!* (a parody issue of *Mind*, published by the editors as a special Christmas number, 1901), pages 87–101.

'The Hunting of the Snark'. Devereux Court. The *Cornhill Magazine*, Volume 30, March 1911, pages 360–65.

'Finding of the Snark'. Arthur Ruhl. *Saturday Review of Literature*, Volume 9, 18 March 1933, pages 490–91.

'1874–76 – The Hunting of the Snark'. Chapter 10, *The Diaries of Lewis Carroll*. Edited by Roger Green. Oxford, 1954.

'The Baker Murder Case'. Larry T. Shaw. *Inside and Science Fiction Advertiser*, September 1956, pages 4–12.

'The Hunting of the Snark'. Richard Howard in *Master Poems of the English Language*. Edited by Oscar Williams. Trident, 1966, pages 773–6.

'Ironic Voyages'. Chapter 4, *Nil: Episodes in the Literary Conquest of Void During the Nineteenth Century*. Robert Martin Adams, Oxford University Press, 1966.

'Snark Hunting: Lewis Carroll on Collectivism'. E. Merrill Root, *American Opinion*, April 1966, pages 73–82.

'What is a Boojum? Nonsense and Modernism.' Michael Holquist, *Yale French Studies*, Volume 43, 1969, pages 145–64. Reprinted in *Alice in Wonderland*, edited by Donald J. Gray, Norton, 1971.

ABOUT LEWIS CARROLL

The Life and Letters of Lewis Carroll. Stuart Dodgson Collingwood, Unwin, 1898.

The Story of Lewis Carroll. Isa Bowman, J. M. Dent, 1899.

Lewis Carroll. Walter de la Mare, Cambridge, 1930.

The Life of Lewis Carroll. Langford Reed, W. & G. Foyle, 1932.

Carroll's Alice. Harry Morgan Ayres, Columbia, 1936.

Victoria Through the Looking-Glass. Florence Becker Lennon, Simon & Schuster, 1945. Collier paperback, 1962.

The Story of Lewis Carroll. Roger Lancelyn Green, Methuen, 1949.

Lewis Carroll: Photographer. Helmut Gernsheim, Chanticleer Press, 1949.

The White Knight. Alexander L. Taylor, Oliver and Boyd, 1952.

Lewis Carroll. Derek Hudson, Constable, 1954.

Swift and Carroll. Phyllis Greenacre, International Universities Press, 1955.

Lewis Carroll. Number 96 of a series of booklets entitled *Writers and Their Work.* Derek Hudson, Longmans, Green, 1958.

Lewis Carroll. Roger Lancelyn Green, Bodley Head, 1960.

The Snark was a Boojum. James Plysted Wood. Illustrated by David Levine. Pantheon, 1966.

Language and Lewis Carroll. Robert D. Sutherland, Mouton, The Hague, 1970.

ABOUT HENRY HOLIDAY

'Henry Holiday and His Art'. Angus M. MacKay. *Westminster Review*, Volume 158, London 1902, pages 391–400.

'The Decorative Work of Mr Henry Holiday'. Unsigned. *International Studio*, Volume 37, New York, 1909, pages 106–15.

Reminiscences of My Life. Henry Holiday. William Heinemann, 1914.

'Henry Holiday'. A. L. Baldry. *Walker's Quarterly*, Numbers 31–2, London 1930, pages 1–80.

APPENDIX

The following commentary, by the pragmatist philosopher F. C. S. Schiller, originally appeared in *Mind!*, a parody issue of *Mind*, a British philosophical journal. The parody was published in 1901 as a special Christmas number and is believed to have been written almost entirely by Schiller. The year 1901 was a time when the great bugaboo of pragmatism was the Hegelian concept of the Absolute, a concept no longer fashionable in philosophic circles, though it continues to be smuggled into Protestant theology by German theologians with Hegelian pasts.

The frontispiece of *Mind!* is a 'Portrait of Its Immanence the Absolute', printed on pink paper, to symbolize the pink of perfection, and protected by a tipped-in sheet of transparent tissue. The editors note the portrait's striking resemblance to the Bellman's map in *The Hunting of the Snark*. Beneath the absolutely blank pink portrait are instructions for use: 'Turn the eye of faith, fondly but firmly on the centre of the page, wink the other, and gaze fixedly until you see It.'

It was this comic issue of *Mind* that provided Bertrand Russell with what he once insisted was the only instance he had ever encountered in which someone actually thought in a formal syllogism. A German philosopher had been much puzzled by the magazine's burlesque advertisements. Finally he reasoned: Everything in this magazine is a joke, the advertisements are in this magazine, therefore the advertisements must be jokes. Footnotes to the commentary are Schiller's except for those that I have added and initialled. – M.G.

A COMMENTARY ON THE *Snark*
Snarkophilus Snobbs
[F. C. S. SCHILLER]

It is a recognized maxim of literary ethics that none but the dead can deserve a commentary, seeing that they can no longer either explain themselves or perturb the explanations of those who devote themselves to the congenial, and frequently not unprofitable, task of making plain what was previously obscure, and profound what was previously plain. Hence it is easily understood that the demise of the late lamented Lewis Carroll has opened a superb field to the labours of the critical commentator, and that the classical beauties of the two *Alices* are not likely long to remain unprovided with those aids to comprehension which the cultivated reader so greatly needs.

The purpose of the present article, however, is a more ambitious one. Most of Lewis Carroll's non-mathematical writings are such that even the dullest of grown-ups can detect, more or less vaguely, their import; but *The Hunting of the Snark* may be said to have hitherto baffled the adult understanding. It is to lovers of Lewis Carroll what *Sordello* is to lovers of Robert Browning, or *The Shaving of Shagpat* to Meredithians. In other words, it has frequently been considered magnificent but not sense. The author himself anticipated the possibility of such criticism and defends himself against it in his preface, by appealing to the 'strong moral purpose' of his poem, to the arithmetical principles it inculcates, to 'its noble teachings in Natural History'. But prefatory explanations are rightly disregarded by the public, and it must be admitted that in Lewis Carroll's case they do but little to elucidate the *Mystery of the Snark*, which, it has been calculated,* has been responsible for 49½ per cent of the cases of insanity and nervous breakdown which have occurred during the last ten years.

It is clear then that a commentary on *The Hunting of the Snark* is the greatest desideratum of English literature at present; and this the author of the present essay flatters himself that he has provided. Not that he would wish the commentary itself to be regarded as ex-

* See the Colney Hatch *Contributions to Sociology* for 1899, p. 983.

Appendix

haustive or as anything more than a *vindemiatio prima* of so fruitful
a subject: but he would distinctly advance the claim to have dis-
covered the key to the real meaning and philosophical significance of
this most remarkable product of human imagination.

What then is the meaning of the *Snark*? Or that we may not appear
to beg the question let us first ask – how do we know that the *Snark*
has a meaning? The answer is simple; Lewis Carroll assures us that it
not only has a meaning but even a moral purpose. Hence we may
proceed with his assurance and our own.

I will not weary you with an autobiographical narrative of the way
in which I discovered the solution of the Snark's mystery; suffice it to
say that insight came to me suddenly, as unto Buddha under the
Bô-tree, as I was sitting under an Arrowroot in a western prairie. The
theory of the Snark which I then excogitated has stood the test of
time, and of a voyage across the Atlantic, in the course of which I was
more than tempted to throw overboard all my most cherished con-
victions, and I have little doubt that when you have heard my
evidence you will share my belief.

I shall begin by stating the general argument of the Snark and pro-
ceed to support it by detailed comment. In the briefest possible
manner, then, I assert that the Snark is the Absolute, dear to pholi-
sophers,* and that the hunting of the Snark is the pursuit of the
Absolute. Even as thus barely stated the theory all but carries in-
stantaneous conviction; it is infinitely more probable than that the
Snark should·be an electioneering device or a treatise on 'society' or
a poetical narrative of the discovery of America, to instance a few of
the fatuous suggestions with which I have been deluged since I began
to inquire into the subject. But further considerations will easily
raise the antecedent probability that the Snark is the Absolute to
certainty. The Absolute, as I venture to remark for the benefit of any
unpholisophical enough still to enjoy that ignorance thereof which is
bliss, is a fiction which is supposed to do for pholisophers everything
they can't do for themselves. It performs the same functions in
philosophy as infinity in mathematics; when in doubt you send for
the Absolute; if something is impossible for us, it is *therefore* possible
for the Absolute; what is nonsense to us is *therefore* sense to the

* A term for Hegelian philosophers, used throughout the comic issue of *Mind*. –
M.G.

Absolute and *vice versa*; what we do not know, the Absolute knows; in short it is the apotheosis of topsyturvydom. Now, Lewis Carroll as a man of sense did not believe in the Absolute, but he recognized that it could best be dealt with in parables.

The Hunting of the Snark, therefore, is intended to describe Humanity in search of the Absolute, and to exhibit the vanity of the pursuit. For no one attains to the Absolute but the Baker, the miserable madman who has left his intelligence behind before embarking. And when he does find the Snark, it turns out to be a Boojum, and he 'softly and silently vanished away'. That is, the Absolute can be attained only by the loss of personality, which is merged in the Boojum. The Boojum is the Absolute, as the One which absorbs the Many, and danger of this is the 'moral purpose' whereof Lewis Carroll speaks so solemnly in his preface. Evidently we are expected to learn the lesson that the Snark will *always* turn out a Boojum, and the dramatic variety of the incidents only serves to lead up to this most thrilling and irreparable catastrophe.

But I proceed to establish this interpretation in detail. (1) We note that the poem has 8 fits. These clearly represent the Time-process in which the Absolute is supposed to be revealed, and at the same time hint that Life as a whole is a *Survival of the Fit*. But why 8 and not 7 or 9? Evidently because by revolving 8 through an angle of 90° it becomes the symbol for Infinity, which is often regarded as an equivalent of the Absolute. (2) The vessel clearly is Humanity and in the crew are represented various human activities by which it is supposed we may aspire to the Absolute. We may dwell a little on the significance of the various members of the crew. They are *ten* in number and severally described as a Bellman, a Butcher, a Banker, a Beaver, a Broker, a Barrister, a Bonnet-maker, a Billiard-marker, a Boots and a Baker. It is obvious that all these names begin with a *B*, and somewhat remarkable that even the Snark turns out a Boojum. This surely indicates that we are here dealing with the most ultimate of all questions, *viz.*, 'to be or not to be', and that it is answered in the universal affirmative – *B* at any cost!

Next let us inquire what these personages represent. In the leading figure, that of the *Bellman* we easily recognize *Christianity*, the bell being the characteristically Christian implement, and the hegemony of humanity being equally obvious. Emboldened by this success, it is easy to make out that the *Butcher* is *Mohammedanism,* and the *Banker Judaism,* while the *Beaver* represents the aspirations of the animals towards τὸ Θεῖον.* The anonymous *Baker* is, of course, the hero of the story, and the 'forty-two boxes all carefully packed with his name painted clearly on each' which he 'left behind on the beach' typify the contents of his mind, which he lost before starting on his quest.

The *Barrister* is clearly the type of the *logician* and brought 'to arrange their disputes'. He too has dreams about the Absolute and wearies himself by proving in vain that the 'Beaver's lacemaking was wrong'; as anyone who has studied modern logic can testify, it does dream about the Absolute and is always 'proving in vain'.

The *Broker* brought 'to value their goods' (ἀγαθά) is evidently *moral philosophy.* The '*Billiard-marker* whose skill was immense' is certainly *Art,* which would grow too engrossing (= 'might perhaps have won more than his share') but for the pecuniary considerations represented by the Banker (Judaism) who 'had the whole of their cash in his care'.

In the *Boots* we can hardly hesitate to recognize *Literature,* which serves to put literary polish upon the outer integuments of the other intellectual pursuits.

The *Bonnet-maker* finally is manifestly the *Fashion,* without which it would have been madness to embark upon so vast an undertaking.

Having thus satisfactorily accounted for the *dramatis personae* I proceed to comment on the action.

F. 1, st. 1.

> 'Just the place for a Snark!' the Bellman cried,
> As he landed his crew with care;
> Supporting each man on the top of the tide
> By a finger entwined in his hair.

The meaning evidently is that Christianity 'touches the highest part of man and supports us from above'.

F. 1, st. 12.

> He would joke with hyænas

---

* Cp. Aristotle, *Eth. Nich.*, vii, 13, 6.

It is well known that few animals have a keener sense of humour than hyenas and that no animal can raise a heartier laugh than the right sort of hyena.

> And he once went a walk, paw-in-paw with a bear

The learned Prof. Grubwitz has discovered a characteristically Teutonic difficulty here. In his monumental commentary on the *Shaving of Shagpat*, he points out that *as human* the Baker had no paws and could not possibly therefore have offered a paw to a bear. Hence he infers that the text is corrupt. The 'w' of the second 'paw' is evidently, he thinks, due to the dittograph initial letter of the succeeding 'with'. The original 'papa' having thus been corrupted into a 'papaw' (a tropical tree not addicted to locomotion), an ingenious scribe inserted 'w-in' giving a specious but mistaken meaning. The original reading was 'papa with a bear', and indicates that a forebear or ancestor was intended. So far Grubwitz, who if he had been more familiar with English slang would doubtless have dealt with the text in a more forbearing and less overbearing manner. Anyhow the difficulty is gratuitous, for it must be admitted that the whole stanza is calculated to give anyone paws.

> 'Just to keep up its spirits,' he said.

It was probably depressed because it could only make a bare living.

In the second Fit the first point of importance would seem to be the Bellman's map. This is manifestly intended for a description of the *Summum Bonum* or Absolute Good, which represents one of the favourite methods of attaining the Absolute. Moreover, as Aristotle shows, a knowledge of the *Summum Bonum* is of great value to humanity in crossing the ocean of life, although its τέλος is οὐ γνῶσις ἀλλὰ πρᾶξις.

F. 2, st. 3.

> 'What's the good of Mercator's North Poles and Equators,
> Tropics, Zones and Meridian Lines?'

These terms evidently ridicule the attempt made in various ways to fill in the conception of the *Summum Bonum*, but I confess I cannot identify the chief philosophic notions in their geographical disguises.

F. 2, st. 6.

> When he cried, 'Steer to starboard, but keep her head larboard!'
> What on earth was the helmsman to do?

The question in the first place is quite irrelevant, as the helmsman was not on earth but at sea and likely to remain there. Still, bearing in mind the effect of this remarkable nautical manoeuvre, we may perhaps make bold to answer: 'He should have turned tail!' For the effect upon the ship would be to make it toss and, as the Bellman obviously preferred the head, the helmsman should have cried 'Tails!'

F. 2, st. 9.

> Yet at first sight the crew were not pleased with the view,
> Which consisted of chasms and crags.

When Humanity first really catches a glimpse of the local habitation of the Absolute in the writings of the pholisophers, it is disappointed and appalled by its 'chasms and crags', i.e., the difficulties and obscurities of these authors' account.

F. 2, st. 10.

> The Bellman perceived that their spirits were low,
> And repeated in musical tone
> Some jokes he had kept for a season of woe –
> But the crew would do nothing but groan.

Tutors have been known to adopt similar methods with a similar effect.

F. 2, st. 15. We now come to what is perhaps the most crucial point in our commentary, namely, 'the five unmistakable marks, by which you may know, wheresoever you go, the warranted Genuine Snarks. Let us take them in order. The first is its taste, which is meagre and hollow, but crisp: like a coat that is rather too tight in the waist, with a flavour of Will-o'-the-wisp.'

 1. The taste of the Snark is the taste for the Absolute, which is not emotionally satisfactory, 'meagre and hollow, but crisp' and hence attractive to the Baker, while the elusiveness of the Absolute sufficiently explains the 'flavour of Will-o'-the-wisp'. Its affinity for 'a

coat that is rather too tight in the waist' applies only to its 'meagre and hollow' character; for unless the coat were hollow you could not get into it, while it would, of course, be meagre or scanty if it were 'too tight in the waist'.

2.   'Its habit of getting up late you'll agree
        That it carries too far, when I say
        That it frequently breakfasts at five-o'clock tea
        And dines on the following day.'

In this the poet shows, in four lines, what many pholisophers have vainly essayed to prove in as many volumes, namely that the Absolute is not, and cannot be, in Time.

3.   'The third is its slowness in taking a jest.
        Should you happen to venture on one,
        It will sigh like a thing that is deeply distressed:
        And it always looks grave at a pun.'

This third characteristic of the Absolute is also found in many of its admirers, I am sorry to say. It is best passed over in silence, as our author says elsewhere, without 'a shriek or a scream, scarcely even a howl or a groan'.

4.   'The fourth is its fondness for bathing-machines,
        Which it constantly carries about,
        And believes that they add to the beauty of scenes –
        A sentiment open to doubt.'

The 'philosophic desperado' in pursuit of Nirvana achieves his fell design by a purificatory plunge into the ocean of Absolute Being. This, however, is not an aesthetic spectacle which 'adds to the beauty of scenes', and hence the Snark obligingly carries bathing-machines about in order that in Mr Gladstone's phrase 'essential decency may be preserved'.

5. 'The fifth is ambition.' The Snark's ambition is to become a Boojum, of course. It always succeeds with those who are prepared to meet it halfway. You will doubtless have noticed that the five unmistakable criteria of Snarkhood we have just considered are all of a spiritual character and throw no light upon its material appearance. The reason no doubt is that our author was aware of the protean

character of the Absolute's outward appearance, and with true scientific caution did not pretend to give an exhaustive description of the various species of Snark. What, however, he does know he is not loath to tell, and so he bids us distinguish 'those that have feathers and bite from those that have whiskers and scratch'. In this it is needless to seek for a causal connexion between the possession of feathers and mordant habits. The fact is simply mentioned to distinguish these Snarks from birds which have feathers but – since the extinction of the *Archaeopteryx* and *Hesperornis* – have long ceased to wear genuine teeth and to bite, and angels which have feathers but don't bite, not because they are physically, but because they are morally, incapable of so doing. Similarly it would be fanciful to connect the scratching, which is attributed to the second kind of Snark, with the possession of whiskers even in an inchoate condition. But *vide infra* for the doubt about the reading.

Let us consider therefore first the information about the outward characteristics of these Snarks. Some have feathers, some have whiskers. There is no difficulty about the former. We simply compare the well-known poem of Emerson on Brahma, in which the latter points out to those who object to being parts of the Absolute, that 'when me they fly I am the wings'. If wings, then probably feathers; for the featherless wings of insects are utterly unworthy of any kind of Snark.

The mention of Snarks with whiskers on the other hand constitutes a difficulty. For we cannot attribute anything so anthropomorphic to the Absolute. There is, however, evidence of a various reading. The Bodleian MS B₂ 48971, which is supposed to be in the author's own handwriting, reads *whiskey* instead of *whiskers*. The change is a slight one, but significant. For we may then compare Spinoza's well-known views about the Absolute, which caused him to be euphemistically described as 'a God-intoxicated man'. It should also be remembered that various narcotics such as bhang, opium, hashish, arrack, etc., have been used to produce the mystic union of the devotee or debauchee with the Absolute, and many hold that whiskey is as good as any of them.

It remains to account for the habit of the Snark in biting and scratching. The learned Grubwitz, to whom allusion has already been made, thinks that these terms are intended to indicate respectively the male and female forms of the Snark (who, in his opinion, represents the university student who is capable of becoming a Boojum – a professor causing all who meet him 'softly and silently to vanish away'). The demonstrable absurdity of his general theory of the Snark encourages me to reject also Grubwitz's interpretation in detail, in spite of my respect for his learning. I should prefer, therefore, to explain the biting and scratching more simply as due to the bad temper naturally engendered in so inordinately hunted an animal.

The Third Fit opens, as the reader will doubtless remember, with the attempts made to restore the fainting Baker.

> They roused him with muffins – they roused him with ice –
> They roused him with mustard and cress –
> They roused him with jam and judicious advice –
> They set him conundrums to guess

Such as, probably, *Riddles of the Sphinx*.* The other means seem to have been injudicious.

Skipping, with the Bellman, the Baker's father and mother, we come to his 'dear uncle', who, *lying* on his deathbed, was able to give the important information which has proved so epoch-making in the history of Snarkology.

And first let us ask who was the 'dear uncle'? In answering this question we not only gratify our scientific curiosity but also discover the name of the Baker, our 'hero unnamed', as he is subsequently (F. 8, st. 4) called. Now, it must be admitted that we are not told the uncle's name either, but I think that from the account given there can be little doubt but that it ought to have been Hegel. Now a distinguished Oxford pholisopher has proved that what may be and ought to be, that ∴ [therefore] is; and so the inference is practically certain.

F. 3, st. 7.

> 'He remarked to me then,' said that mildest of men,
> ' "If your Snark be a Snark, that is right:
> Fetch it home by all means – you may serve it with
>   greens' – T. H. Green's † to wit –
> 'And it's handy for striking a light." '

* The title of F. C. S. Schiller's best-known book. – M.G.

† Thomas Hill Green was a distinguished Neo-Hegelian philosopher at Balliol College, Oxford. – M.G.

It is well known that Hegel thought that the *wrong* kind of Absolute (that of the other professors) was 'like the night in which all cows are black'. It follows that the right kind – his own – would conversely serve as an illuminant.

F. 3, st. 8.

> ' "You may seek it with thimbles – and seek it with care;
> You may hunt it with forks and hope;
> You may threaten its life with a railway-share;
> You may charm it with smiles and soap –" '

'You may seek it with thimbles' – this passage is repeated in F. 4, st. 8, by the Bellman, whose subsequent remark in st. 10, 'To rig yourselves out for the fight,' explains its meaning. Evidently Lewis Carroll here meant subtly to suggest that the pursuit of the Absolute was a form of intellectual *thimble-rigging*.

'You may hunt it with forks and hope.' Just as only the brave can deserve the fair, so only the *forktunate* can *hope* to attain the Absolute. There is no justification for depicting Care and Hope as allegorical females joining in the hunt, as the illustrator has done. Altogether the serious student cannot be too emphatically warned against this plausible impostor's pictures; they have neither historic authority nor philosophic profundity. He attributes, e.g., a Semitic physiognomy to the Broker instead of to the Banker; he persistently represents the Baker as clean-shaven and bald, in spite of the statement (in F. 4, st. 11) that 'The Baker with care combed his whiskers and hair,' and his picture of the Snark exhibits neither feathers nor whiskers! 'You may threaten its life with a railway-share.' This alludes to the deleterious effect of modern enlightenment and modern improvements on the vitality of the Absolute. 'You may charm it with smiles and soap.' I.e. adulation and ascetic practices, soap being the substance most abhorrent to Fakirs and Indian sages generally, and therefore suggesting the highest degree of asceticism.

But after all, the momentous revelation of the Baker's uncle is neither his account of the methods of hunting the Snark – they are commonplace enough and he evidently did not choose to divulge his own patent of the Dialectical Method – nor yet his account of the use to which the Absolute may be put – it is trivial enough in all conscience – but rather the possibility – nay, as in the light of subsequent

113

events we must call it, the certainty – that the Snark is a Boojum. No wonder that even the dauntless Baker could not endure the thought that if he met with a Boojum he would 'softly and suddenly vanish away', and that the Bellman 'looked uffish, and wrinkled his brow'. He was of course bound to conceal his emotions and to take an uffishial view of the dilemma. So his reproaches are temperate –

> 'But surely, my man, when the voyage began,
> You might have suggested it then?'
>
> 'It's excessively awkward to mention it now –'

F. 4, st. 5.

> 'I said it in Hebrew – I said it in Dutch –
> I said it in German and Greek;
> But I wholly forgot (and it vexes me much)
> That English is what you speak!'

The accounts of the Absolute in German and Greek are famous, while the Hebrew and Dutch probably both refer to Spinoza, who was a Dutch Jew, though he wrote in bad Latin. The forgetting to speak (and write) English is a common symptom in the pursuit of the Absolute.

F. 4, st. 14.

> While the Billiard-marker with quivering hand
> Was chalking the tip of his nose.

Art, when brought face to face with the imminence of the Absolute, recoils upon itself.

The argument of the Fifth Fit is broadly this, that the Butcher and the Beaver both hit upon the same method of approaching the Absolute, by way of the higher mathematics, and so become reconciled. Into the reason of this coincidence, and the rationality of this method it boots not to inquire, the more so as it proved abortive, and neither of them were destined to discover the Snark. That they were brought together, however, by their common fear of the *Jubjub Bird* is interesting, and could doubtless be explained if we could determine the meaning of that volatile creature.

Let us ask, then, what is the Jubjub? In reply I shall dismiss, with the brevity which is the soul both of wit and contempt, the preposterous suggestion that the Jubjub is the pelican. But I am free to confess that I have spent many a sleepless night over the Jubjub. Philologically, indeed it was not difficult to discover that Jubjub is a 'portmanteau bird', compounded of *jabber* and *jujube*, but even this did not seem at first to give much of a clue to the problem. Finally, however, it struck me that the author had, with the true prescience and generosity of genius, himself stated the solution of the riddle in the line immediately preceding his description of the Jubjub. It is –

> Would have caused quite a thrill in Society

It flashed across me that the Jubjub was Society itself, and if I may quote the account of the Jubjub's habits it will be seen how perfectly this solution covers the facts.

> 'As to temper the Jubjub's a desperate bird,
> Since it lives in perpetual passion:'

This describes the desperate struggle and rush which prevails in Society.

> 'Its taste in costume is entirely absurd –
> It is ages ahead of the fashion:'

How profoundly true this is! To be in Society this is what we must aim at; we can never be in fashion unless we are ahead of the fashion.

> 'But it knows any friend it has met *once* before:'

It is most important in Society to remember the people you have met even once, alike whether you intend to recognize them or to cut them; otherwise vexatious mistakes will occur. There is subtle sarcasm also in the use of the term 'friend' to describe such chance acquaintances.

> 'It never will look at a bribe:'

Such is its anxiety to pocket it.

> 'And in charity-meetings it stands at the door,
> And collects – though it does not subscribe.'

No one who has ever had anything to do with charity bazaars can fail to recognize this!

'Its flavour when cooked is more exquisite far
Than mutton, or oysters, or eggs:'

The taste for Society is of all the most engrossing.

('Some think it keeps best in an ivory jar,
And some, in mahogany kegs:')

Some think Society appears to best advantage in an ivory jar, i.e., a 'crush' of *décolletées* women, others at a dinner party over the mahogany board.

'You boil it in sawdust: you salt it in glue:'

Dust is American slang for money, so *sawdust* is but *metri gratia* for sordid-dust. That is, Society is boiled, i.e., raised to the effervescence of the greatest excitement, by filthy lucre. 'You salt it in glue.' *Salt* is short for 'to captivate by putting salt on its tail', *glue* is put metaphorically for *adhesiveness*, and the whole, therefore, means that Society is captured by pertinacity.

'You condense it with locusts and tape:'

I.e., lest it should become too thin, you thicken it with parasitic 'diners out' to amuse it, and officials (addicted to red tape) to lend it solemnity.

'Still keeping one principal object in view,
To preserve its symmetrical shape.'

The importance of keeping the proper 'form' of Society intact is too obvious to need comment. It is hardly necessary to add also that the reluctance of the Mohammedan and the animal to face a society in which the female sex dominates to such an extent fully explains their common fear of the Jubjub. Lastly it is clear that a word compounded of *jabber* and *jujubes*, the latter being used metaphorically for all unwholesome delights, Turkish and otherwise, is a very judicious description of Society.

The Sixth Fit is occupied with the interlude of the Barrister's dream, which seems to have been prophetic in character and throws further light on the Absolute. That Logic should dream of the Absolute will not of course surprise those who have followed the recent aberrations of the subject. Let us consider then this dream of Logic's.

F. 6, st. 3.

> He dreamed that he stood in a shadowy Court,
> Where the Snark, with a glass in its eye,
> Dressed in gown, bands, and wig, was defending a pig
> On the charge of deserting its sty.

The pig was probably *Epicuri de grege porcus*, and the charge of deserting its sty was a charge of pig-sticking or *suicide*. For, as the divine Plato excellently shows in the *Phaedo* (62 B), to commit suicide is to desert one's post, and so to desert the *four* posts of the pigsty must be still worse.

F. 6, st. 4.

> The Witnesses proved, without error or flaw,
> That the sty was deserted when found:
> And the Judge kept explaining the state of the law
> In a soft under-current of sound.

The Judge is *Conscience*, the exponent of the Moral Law, noted for its still small voice.

F. 6, st. 6.

> The Jury had each formed a different view
> (Long before the indictment was read),
> And they all spoke at once, so that none of them knew
> One word that the others had said.

The Jury is *Public Opinion* which was evidently (as so often) very much perplexed by the pigculiarities of the case.

F. 6, st. 7.

> 'You must know –' said the Judge: but the Snark exclaimed 'Fudge!
> That statute is obsolete quite!
> Let me tell you, my friends, the whole question depends
> On an ancient manorial right.'

The question was whether the pig was free, or *ascriptus harae*, justly 'penned in its pen'. In other words, does being born involve a moral obligation to remain alive?

F. 6, st. 8.

> 'In the matter of Treason the pig would appear
> To have aided, but scarcely abetted:'

For a soldier to desert his post is, or may be, treason; hence the charge of treason against the suicide.

> 'While the charge of Insolvency fails, it is clear,
> If you grant the plea "never indebted".'

The suicide is accused of insolvency, of failing to meet the obligations which life imposes on him. His reply is 'never indebted', he owes life nothing, he received no 'stipend' and will not be 'sued for a debt he never did contract'.

F. 6, st. 9.

> 'The fact of Desertion I will not dispute,
> But its guilt, as I trust, is removed
> (So far as relates to the costs of this suit)
> By the *Alibi* which has been proved.'

You prove an *alibi* by not being there. The pig's defence was that it was not there or not all there; in other words, not *compos mentis*. That is, the old excuse of temporary insanity!

F. 6, st. 11.

> But the Judge said he never had summed up before;
> So the Snark undertook it instead,

Conscience has to pronounce judgment upon the particular case, but this particular case has never occurred before; hence Conscience finds itself unable to decide and leaves the matter to the Absolute. The attitude of Public Opinion is similar: 'when the verdict was called for, the Jury declined', and 'ventured to hope that the Snark wouldn't mind undertaking that duty as well'.

In the end the Absolute not only has to defend the offender and take his guilt upon Itself, but also, as ἓν καὶ πᾶν, to assume all the other functions as well, to find the verdict and to pronounce the sentence. Its readiness to do this is suspicious, and suggests the idea that it was acting collusively throughout in pretending to defend the pig.

'So the Snark *found* the verdict,' *where* we are not told, but *what* we might have anticipated.

> When it said the word 'GUILTY!' the Jury all groaned,
> And some of them fainted away.

The verdict involved a shock to enlightened Public Opinion, like that of the Dreyfus case. The sentence after that seemed comparatively light and so was received with approval.

> 'Transportation for life' was the sentence it gave,
> 'And *then* to be fined forty pound.'
> The Jury all cheered, though the Judge said he feared
> That the phrase was not legally sound.

The sentence was of course absurd, for the suicide had already transported himself out of jurisdiction.

F. 6, st. 16.

> But their wild exultation was suddenly checked
> When the jailer informed them, with tears,
> Such a sentence would have not the slightest effect,
> As the pig had been dead for some years.

The jailer, whose duty it is to keep the pigs in their styes, is the *doctor* After all, you can do nothing with a *successful* suicide.

F. 6, st. 17.

> The Judge left the Court, looking deeply disgusted:
> But the Snark, though a little aghast,
> As the lawyer to whom the defence was intrusted,
> Went bellowing on to the last.

Though such events shock the Conscience, the Absolute is unabashed.

The Seventh Fit is devoted to the Banker's fate and is perhaps the most prophetic of any. For no discerning reader of this commentary can fail to recognize that it forecasts the encounter of Judaism with

119

Anti-Semiticism. Let us follow the description of this disgraceful episode in contemporary history.

F. 7, st. 3.

> A Bandersnatch swiftly drew nigh
> And grabbed at the Banker, who shrieked in despair,
> For he knew it was useless to fly.
>
> He offered large discount – he offered a cheque
> (Drawn to 'bearer') for seven-pounds-ten:
> But the Bandersnatch merely extended its neck
> And grabbed at the Banker again.

The Anti-Semitic Bandersnatch shows that it cannot be bribed by insufficient 'ransom', and that two can play at a game of grab.

> Without rest or pause – while those frumious jaws
> Went savagely snapping around –
> He skipped and he hopped, and he floundered and flopped,
> Till fainting he fell to the ground.

After the Anti-Semitic rioters had been driven off, it was found that the Banker –

> ... was black in the face, and they scarcely could trace
> The least likeness to what he had been:
> While so great was his fright that his waistcoat turned white –
> A wonderful thing to be seen!

This alludes to the wonderful affinity Judaism has for clothing, and we may parallel this passage by referring to Shakespeare's (?) *Merchant of Venice*, Act ii., Scene 1. There an insult offered to his 'Jewish gaberdine' produces a powerful emotional effect upon Shylock. Here conversely the ill treatment of their wearer calls forth a sympathetic compensatory effect on the part of the clothes.

In the Eighth Fit the tragedy reaches its consummation and comment is almost needless.

It must be *read*, not without tears, and every line in it confirms the view we have taken of the Snark.

F. 8, st. 5.

> Erect and sublime, for one moment of time.

I.e., before becoming a moment in the timeless Absolute.

F. 8, st. 9.

> In the midst of the word he was trying to say,
> In the midst of his laughter and glee,
> He had softly and silently vanished away –*
> For the Snark *was* a Boojum you see.

One can't help feeling a little sorry for the Baker personally, but nevertheless the verdict of Philosophy must be: 'So perish all who brave the Snark again!'

* This line is persistently misquoted by Snobbs; the word is *suddenly*, not *silently*. – M.G.

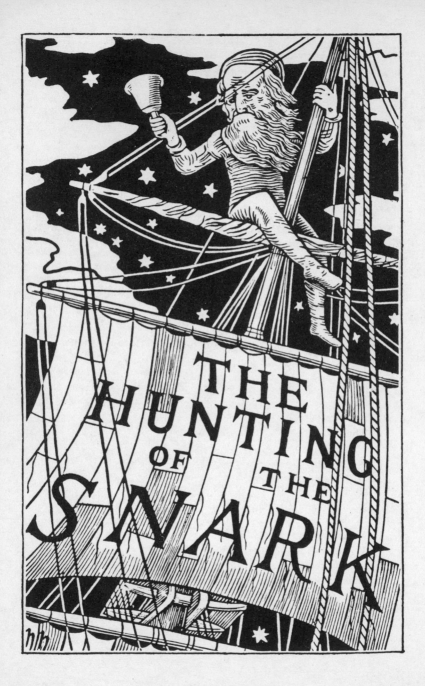

THE HUNTING OF THE SNARK

FIT THE SEVEN-AND-A-HALFTH

THE CLUE

J. A. LINDON, whose name has been mentioned many times in the notes, is the author of the following fit.

It is rather disappointing [he writes in a letter] that we hear so little of some of the other members of the crew. Further, one feels that the violence of the Banker's Fate detracts from the drama of the ending, the Vanishing, which follows it. So, just for amusement, I have concocted an extra fit, which we can imagine as coming between these two concluding fits. It is of average length and (as befits interpolation, and especially one at that point) it is not violent or particularly dramatic. Nobody meets a decisive fate, and neither the balance of the tale nor the general status quo is altered.

Mr Lindon's fit fits so neatly into the spirit of Carroll's agony that I think it provides this fitful commentary with a most fitting conclusion.

> THEY sought it with thimbles, they sought it with care;
>   They pursued it with forks and hope;
> They threatened its life with a railway-share;
>   They charmed it with smiles and soap.
>
> But the Billiard-marker, who'd left on the ship
>   All the cannons he'd recently made,
> Had wandered apart, with the red in his grip,
>   To a spot of convenient shade.
>
> Where, baulked of all hope, he was potting the soap
>   With the butt of his thimble-tipped cue.
> (In the glummering* dark, with no sign of a Snark,
>   There was not very much he could do.)

* *Glummering* – the sort of gloomy glimmering that makes you glum.

But as he bent, aiming to pocket his care,
  There came a sharp sound in the woods;
And out, all dishevelled, a bow in his hair,
  Flew the maker of Bonnets and Hoods.

He was red with exertion, and blue with the cold,
  He was white with some terror he'd seen;
As the low setting sun turned his feathers to gold
  And his ears a bright emerald green.

He struggled to speak, but emitted a squeak
  Like a bone that has come out of joint.
What on earth had occurred? He had seen – he had heard –
  Not a thing could he do but to point.

The Billiard-marker cajoled him with nods,
  He spun him a kiss off the cush;
He played him a thousand up, giving him odds
  Of nine hundred, not barring the 'push'.

But no word could he say, merely gestured away
  With a frantic but eloquent poke;
So, with tables* and chalk, they set off at a walk,
  For the thing was too grave for a joke.

The sunlight was gilding the tops of the crags,
  The gulfs were all shadowed in blue,
As they heard from afar, like the tearing of rags,
  A sound that they both of them knew.

' 'Tis a Snark!' cried the Billiard-marker with glee,
  ' 'Tis the voice of a Snark!' he exclaimed;
' 'Tis a Snark! Now the times I have told you are three!'
  And with 'jump' for a hazard he aimed.

---

* There was really only one table, but it had a second playing surface under-
neath, in case it rained. The bowsprit generally wobbled on wet days, because the
Billiard-marker used all the ship's glue to keep the balls in position.

The maker of Hoods, quite approving of that,
　　Here showed him a print on the ground:
It was long, it was large, it was dim, it was flat,
　　It was gray, it was new, it was round.

' 'Tis the trail of a Snark!' cried the man who would mark
　　Up the score and put chalk on the cues.
'More than one has been past – when you meet them at last,
　　Snarks are often discovered in twos.'

With forks at the ready, impaling their soap,
　　With threatening shares and a smile,
They followed the tracks with ebullient hope
　　Through the fortieth part of a mile.

Then the maker of Bonnets beribboned his heels,
　　Explaining by signs how he'd seen
Other marks, which had surely been made by the wheels
　　Of a Snarked-about bathing-machine.

They had come to a place among lowering crags,
　　And the sound they were seeking was there:
Like a swishing and scraping, or tearing of rags –
　　'Twas the noise of the Snark in its lair!

They rounded a rock, full of joy at the catch,
　　And there were the creatures quite plain:
One was turning a grindstone, with whirring and scratch,
　　And sucking the crook of his cane.

The other had rolled up the sleeves of his shirt
　　And with scraper and brush well aloft,
He was slaving away at removing the dirt
　　From a shoe that the Broker had doffed.

Like gold in the sun shone the crags every one,
　　Dark-shadowed lay boulders and roots;
From afar in a dell came the sound of the bell;
　　They had only been following – *Boots*.